POINT MAN

How a Man Can Lead a Family

POINT MAN

Steve Farrar

MULTNOMAH

Portland, Oregon 97266

For speaking and conference information, write or call:

Steve Farrar
Strategic Living Ministries
8333 Douglas Avenue
Suite 950 LB#22
Dallas, Texas 75225
Phone: (214) 361-5511

Unless otherwise indicated, all Scripture references are from the Holy Bible: New International Version, © 1973, 1978, 1984 by the International Bible Society. Used by permission of Zondervan Bible Publishers.

Scripture references marked NASB are from the New American Standard Bible, The Lockman Foundation © 1960, 1962, 1963, 1968, 1971, 1972, 1973, 1975, 1977. Used by permission.

Scripture references marked TLB are from The Living Bible, © 1971 by Tyndale House Publishers, Wheaton, Ill. Used by permission.

Scripture references marked Phillips are from J. B. Phillips: The New Testament in Modern English, revised edition. J. B. Phillips © 1958, 1960, 1972. Used by permission of Macmillan Publishing Co., Inc.

Cover design by Durand Demlow
Edited by Steve Halliday and Larry Libby
Author photograph by Victor Petersen

POINT MAN
© 1990 by Steve Farrar
Published by Multnomah Press
10209 SE Division Street
Portland, Oregon 97266

Multnomah Press is a ministry of
Multnomah School of the Bible
8435 NE Glisan Street
Portland, Oregon 97220

Printed in the United States of America.

Library of Congress Cataloging-in-Publication Data

Farrar, Steve.
    Point man : how a man can lead a family / Steve Farrar.
        p.   cm.
    Includes bibliographical references.
    ISBN 0-88070-515-9
        1. Fathers—Religious life.   2. Parenting—Religious aspects—
    Christianity.   I. Title.
    BV4846.F36   1990
    248.8'421—dc20   90-37435
                                                                            CIP

92   93   94   95   96   97 - 6   5

Dedication

To
James R. Farrar,
my dad,
in appreciation for over forty years
of spiritual leadership
where it really counts.
At home.

Contents

Acknowledgments

In 1977, I had lunch with Ray Stedman at the Elks Club in Palo Alto, California. Ray has been pastor of Peninsula Bible Church since 1951. I was a twenty-seven-year-old rookie pastor in my first church.

As we were talking, I mentioned my interest in writing. Ray, who has published numerous books, was very encouraging. Then he said, "Steve, let me offer you some advice. Don't publish until you're forty." In that moment, I saw my entire life pass before my eyes. *Thirteen years?* That sounded like an eternity. Now it's here. And so is the book. I only have one question, Ray. Am I supposed to wait another forty years to write another one?

A number of people played strategic roles in enabling this book to become a reality.

• Thanks to Dennis Rainey for his encouragement and support of this project from the very start.

• Dr. John Reed, Scott Ford, and David Martin, along with his excellent staff at Sygnis, were all key players in the early stages.

• Thanks to Stu Weber for recounting his own combat experiences in Vietnam for me. Stu described the experience of going on patrol in such vivid detail that I felt I had been there with him.

• Charlie Boyd, Doug Daily, and the men of Grace Community Church willingly participated as I test-marketed these concepts in the spring of 1989. Their feedback and input were extremely valuable. Charlie, Don Lewis, Jay Werth, Dennis Eenigenburg, and Jeff Farrar each took the time to make astute evaluations of the manuscript.

• Special thanks to the team at Multnomah. Larry Libby and Brenda Jose provided an initial chemistry that was hard to resist. John Van Diest had the vision to go for it, and Larry and Steve Halliday supplied the editorial spit and polish. Tim Kimmel told me you guys were sharp!

• Rachel, John, and Joshua Farrar, three of the best kids in the United States of America, were extremely patient and understanding as Dad wrote "The Book." They gave me valuable help and assistance all the way from page 1 to the very end.

• My mother, Beverly Farrar, covered the domestic bases at our house for two weeks while Mary, Josh, and I were all recovering from a mutant form of mononucleosis—and I was facing a deadline. Thanks for coming through in the clutch, Mom. Once again.

• My wife, Mary, is the Most Valuable Player of this entire project. Come to think of it, she's the MVP of my entire life. Proverbs asks the question, "An excellent wife, who can find?" I did.

CHAPTER ONE

Point Man
on Patrol

It is harder to lead a family than to rule a nation.
Chinese proverb

Albert Einstein was invited to speak at a banquet held in his honor at Swarthmore College. Hundreds of people from all over the country crowded an auditorium to hear what he had to say. When it came time for him to speak, the great physicist walked to the lectern, solemnly looked around, and said, "Ladies and gentlemen, I am very sorry, *but I have nothing to say.*"

Then he sat down. The audience was in shock. A few seconds later, Einstein got up, walked back to the podium, and spoke again. "In case I have something to say, I will come back and say it." Six months later, he wired the president of the college with the message: "Now I have something to say." Another dinner was held, and Einstein made his speech.[1]

A few years ago, I spoke at a Family Life Conference in Irvine, California. More than five hundred men crowded the auditorium. My subject that morning was "Effective Male Leadership in the Home." I talked about the importance of being a committed husband and a tuned-in father. My time with those men was relatively brief, less than an hour.

When I finished my talk, both the usual and the unusual occurred. The usual thing was that several men made their way to the stage to talk with me. Some had questions, some had comments, some just wanted clarification on a point. But then the unusual happened. The first man asked me a question that I had never been asked. Then another man came up and asked me the same question. Then another walked up and said the same thing. In the span of five minutes, close to fifteen people asked me the identical question. One right after the other.

That was unusual.

After hearing a talk on the importance of men becoming effective leaders in their homes, fifteen men came up to me and asked: "What have you written on this?" I had no answer for these men. Like Einstein, I had nothing to say. At least nothing that would fill a book.

But it started me thinking. Thereafter, whenever I spoke on the subject of effective male leadership in the home—whether in Phoenix, Boston, Dallas, Minneapolis, or Boise—I would get the same inquiries:

"What have you written on this?" And my answer was always the same. "Nothing." But at some point I paused and said, "But if I ever do have something to say, I'll let you know."

I now have something to say.

This is a book for men. It's a book for men that talks about *how* to become an effective leader in your home. After three years of research and study, it is my conclusion that effective male leadership in the homes of America is going the way of the dinosaur. Some people are worried about the extinction of whales, condors, snail-darters, or baby seals. Those are legitimate concerns. But let me shoot straight with you. I'm a lot more worried about the extinction of the men who know how to lead a family. And the effective male leader who knows how to lead his family is already on the endangered species list.

In 1980, Dr. James Dobson put it this way: "The Western world stands at a great crossroads in its history. It is my opinion that our very survival as a people will depend upon the presence or absence of masculine leadership in millions of homes . . . I believe, with everything within me, that husbands hold the keys to the preservation of the family."[2]

Things have not gotten any better in the years since Dobson made that statement. If anything, the crisis has grown even more acute.

I now have something to say. Three things, to be specific. And I want to say them to men—men who love their families, who care for their families, and who would die for their families.

War Has Been Declared on the Biblical Family

It's 1966. You are only eighteen. You are in the absolute prime of youth. You've got a driver's license, a girlfriend, and plenty of dreams. Your entire life is ahead of you. But through a strange series of circumstances you don't fully understand, suddenly your driver's license is useless, your girlfriend's picture is in your wallet, your dreams are on hold, and you are in a country thousands of miles away from home.

Welcome to Vietnam.

On this particular day, you would give anything not to be here. For you are going out on patrol. You've been on patrol before, but today is different, and that's why there's a knot in your gut and an icy fear in your heart.

Today is different because the patrol leader has appointed *you* to be "point man." In essence, you're the leader. Everyone else will fall in behind you. And as you move out to encounter the enemy, you realize that the survival of those seven men stepping cautiously behind you will depend upon just one thing: your ability to lead. Your judgment may determine whether they live or die. The responsibility hangs over your head like the suffocating humidity that hangs heavy in the air.

Your senses have never been so alive, your adrenalin so surging. You can almost hear it rushing through your veins. You know the enemy is near, maybe just hundreds of yards away. Intelligence reported heavy enemy activity in this area late last night. Your job is to confirm or deny that activity. For all you know, they're watching you right now. Perhaps they can see you, but you don't have a clue where they are.

As you gingerly make your way through the rain forest, you've got one eye out for concealed wires in your path and another scanning the trees for snipers. Entire patrols have been lost because the point man failed to anticipate an ambush. Men have been killed or horribly maimed, all because a point lacked skill and wisdom.

You never saw it coming. The violent shock and utter surprise of gunfire momentarily paralyzes you, despite your "instant reaction" training. Before you can respond, a bullet tears through your flesh and explodes the bone in your leg. A thousand thoughts instantly flood your mind: *Am I going to die? Where are those shots coming from? Is there more than one? Will I lose my leg? Where's the patrol leader?*

One glance to your left tells you that the family of the patrol leader is now fatherless. In the chaos of attack, and in spite of your wounds, the radio man makes his way to you. He knows and you know that you are the most experienced man. In panic situations like this, the book goes out the window. Like it or not, you are the leader.

As a medic evaluates your wound, you're trying to determine what to do next. Just what is the situation? What are we up against? Where are they? Some good news in the midst of confusion brings a ray of hope—the bullet went through cleanly and the bleeding has stopped. You're luckier than most guys on point. Usually, they're dead before they hit the ground. You're still alive and in control of your thinking.

Two other men beside the patrol leader were hit. One is dead, the other bleeding profusely. You get on the radio and report your situation and position. You request a chopper for the hemorrhaging private. But before you can finish your request, the hidden enemy unleashes all of his firepower on your position. You're surrounded.

In your gut, you know the odds are against you. You're outnumbered, outgunned, and not in the greatest position to wage a counterattack. You've got two men dead, one dying, and four wondering if they'll make it to lunch. The worst case scenario has happened . . . and it's worse than you ever imagined.

Now is the time your leadership will make the difference. What you say and do will determine whether your men live or die. As automatic weapons blaze around you, you must accurately assess the situation, determine the critical next steps, and formulate a flawless plan. It's leadership, pure and simple. If your plan works, you may get out alive with half your men. If it doesn't, they'll be lucky to find your dogtags.

Some of you reading this didn't have to use your imaginations. You were actually there. You know what it is to see your buddy disappear forever into the zippered confines of a body bag. You know first-hand the white-hot heat of phosphorous grenades and the adrenalin rush of a firefight. You know what it's like to be disoriented by the concussion of artillery shells crashing in around you. You don't have to imagine patrolling in Vietnam . . . it's all you can do to get a night's sleep without reliving it again and again.

Let's make a critical change in the scenario. You're still in Vietnam, on patrol in the same steamy rain forest. But something about this patrol is different. You're still the point man, but this time you're not leading a group of men.

You're leading your family.

You look over your shoulder to see your wife and your children following behind. Your little girl is trying to choke back the tears, and your little boy is trying to act brave. Your wife is holding the baby and trying to keep him quiet. On this patrol, you don't want to engage the enemy, you want to avoid him.

What would you be feeling under such conditions? The survival of each member of your family—and its survival as a whole—would completely depend upon your ability to lead through the maze of possible ambushes, unseen booby traps, invisible snipers, and all the extraordinary hazards of combat.

Would you be motivated? Would your senses and adrenalin be working overtime? Of course they would! You would know in your gut that the survival of your family is up to you. It's all on your shoulders . . . because you are the leader.

Gentlemen, this is no imaginary situation. It is reality. If you are a husband/father, then you are in a war. War has been declared upon the family, on your family and mine. *Leading a family through the chaos of American culture is like leading a small patrol through enemy-occupied territory.* And the casualties in this war are as real as the names etched on the Vietnam Memorial.

If you doubt such a war now rages in our country, take another look at the casualty list:

- One out of two marriages ends in divorce.

- The median age for divorce is thirty-four for men and thirty for women.

• In 1960, one out every ten households was maintained by a woman with no husband present; in 1986, one out of every six households was maintained by a woman with no husband present.

• Tonight, enough teenagers to fill the Rose Bowl, Cotton Bowl, Sugar Bowl, Orange Bowl, Fiesta Bowl, and the average Super Bowl will practice prostitution to support drug addictions.

• One million teenage girls will get pregnant out of wedlock this year.

• Five hundred thousand of those girls will abort their babies.

• Of all the fourteen-year-old girls alive today, 40 percent will become pregnant by their nineteenth birthday.

• Sixty percent of all church-involved teenagers are sexually active.

• Sixty-six percent of American high school seniors have used illegal drugs.

• Every seventy-eight seconds, a teenager in America attempts suicide.[3]

Let me ask you something. What are you doing to keep your marriage off the casualty list? You've seen divorce hit your friends and maybe even your extended family. Why won't it happen to you?

It has happened to some of you. You know what it is to have your patrol ambushed. You never saw it coming, but as a result of the enemy's attack, you've lost your marriage and your family. Some of you are still healing from that painful experience, even as you read these pages. I commend you and admire you for picking up this book.

Some of the most teachable people I meet are those who have endured the heartbreak of a divorce. Many of these men and women *never* want to repeat that experience. Because of their painful wounds, they soak up the truth of Scripture like thirsty sponges.

This book will offer some principles to help you avoid another ambush in the future should you re-marry. Some of you already have remarried and are dealing now with all the intricacies of leading a blended family. You are back on patrol. If that is your situation, then this book is for you. Others of you are parenting solo—the toughest job in America. I think you will find some encouraging words in these pages as well. I commend all of you men who have been through a family ambush for taking the time to equip yourself for the ongoing battle against the enemy. God will honor your teachability.

I've asked you how you intend to keep your mar-riage off the casualty list. Let me ask you something else. What are you doing to keep your *kids* off the casu-alty list? Not what is your wife doing, not what is the church youth director doing, not what is the pastor doing, but what are *you* doing? Because some of those kids on that casualty list are from Christian homes.

Some of you have teenagers, and you don't have to be convinced there's a war going on out there. You see the casualties nearly everyday.

But the rest of us don't have teenagers—yet. Let me ask you another question. How long before your kids hit thirteen? How much time do you have left? Two years? Five, maybe ten?

Time is slipping through our fingers like Jell-O in the hands of a two-year-old. We must be actively working to prepare our children to defend themselves against the snipers, ambushes, and booby traps of this silent war. This *is* war, and there are no guarantees our children will stay off the casualty list. But with God's help and our concerned leadership, we can greatly reduce the risks.

It's like the risk of heart attack. None of us have any guarantees we won't suffer a cardiac arrest. Yet at the same time, it is also true that if a man quits smoking, watches his weight, begins some type of aerobic exercise, and stays away from high-fat, high-cholesterol foods, he will greatly reduce his risk of heart attack.

It's the same with our kids. There are no guarantees. You could do everything right, and your child could still rebel and pursue a life of drugs, promiscuity, and irresponsibility. But by consciously, constantly building moral strength into your child's life, you greatly reduce the risk of that happening in the teenage years.

War has been declared on the biblical family. But I have something else I want to say.

Satan Has Two Specific Goals in His War on the Family

In Scripture, God gave us a blueprint for how the family is to function. The father is head of the family. Together with his wife, he raises his children in a home where Jesus Christ is the focus. The Bible is the most important book in the home. It is the responsibility of the parents, and ultimately that of the father, to make sure the children grow up in an environment that will enable them to one day become competent, responsible parents in their own right. This ensures the continuity of the biblical family for the next generation.

It is abundantly clear that one of the goals of the enemy is to interrupt this link of biblical families from generation to generation. He does this by implementing two strategies:

Strategy #1: *To effectively alienate and sever a husband's relationship with his wife.*

Such a division can either be physical or emotional. Both are equally effective.

Strategy #2: *To effectively alienate and sever a father's relationship with his children.*

Again, such a division can either be physical or emotional. Both are equally effective.

A friend of mine, Dave Johnson, is a policeman in San Jose, California. One morning, he was called to the scene of a family disturbance. When he arrived, he found another family that would soon be added to the casualty list:

> The woman was crying and yelling at her husband who was standing with his hands in the pockets of greasy overalls. I noticed homemade tattoos on his arm, usually a sign that someone had been in prison. I was glad that my "fill unit" had arrived. I stepped from my patrol car. As I walked towards the two I could hear the woman yelling at her husband to fix whatever he had done to the car so she could leave. He made no reply, but

only laughed at her with a contemptuous laugh. She turned to me and asked me to make him fix the car. My fill unit broke in and we "split" the two up so that we could find a solution to the problem. I began talking to the husband who said that his wife was having an affair and she was leaving. I asked him if they had gone for counseling and he said that he was not interested.

He went on to say that he was interested in only getting his "things" back. He said that his wife had hidden them from him. I asked his wife about his things and she said she wouldn't give them to him until she got one of the three VCRs they owned. I found out later that his "things" consisted of the narcotics he dealt in. The other officer went to the wife's car and began looking under the hood to see if he could spot the trouble. The husband walked over, took the coil from his pocket, and handed it to the officer. He then told his wife that she could have one of the VCRs if he could have his things. She finally agreed and went into the house. As she entered the house, I noticed two little girls standing in the doorway, watching the drama unfold. They were about eight and ten years old. Both wore dresses and clung to a Cabbage Patch doll. At their feet were two small suitcases. My eyes couldn't leave their faces as they watched the two people they loved tear each other apart.

The woman emerged with the VCR in her arms and went to the car where she put it into the crowded back seat. She turned and told her husband where he could find his things. They both agreed that they had equal shares of the things they had accumulated in ten years of marriage. Then as I stood in unbelief, I watched the husband point to the two little girls and say to the wife, "Well, which one do you want?" Without any apparent emotion, the mother chose the older one. The girls looked at each other as the older one picked up her suitcase and then climbed into her mother's car. I had to stand and watch as the littlest girl, still clutching her Cabbage Patch doll in one hand and her suitcase in the other, watched her big sister and her mother drive off. I watched as tears streamed down her face in total bewilderment. The only "comfort" she received was an order from her father to go into the house as he turned to talk with some friends. There I stood, the unwilling witness to the death of a family.[4]

Families are dying all over America. They are dying on my street and on yours. And in every one of these dead homes, the autopsy would be the same. Cause of death: Strategy #1.

The enemy cannot kill a family without dividing the husband and wife, so that is where he puts his efforts. And it is working. It's a strategy that's been around for thousands of years. It's called divide and conquer.

But there's a flip side to the story. When a husband and wife refuse to allow anything to divide them, they become an impregnable force in the war on the family. When emotional energies are not spent on fighting one another, they can then be used *constructively* . . . to build up their children.

Joe White is a living legend in Christian camping. His outstanding camps in Missouri draw more than five thousand kids from more than forty states. The vast majority of them come from Christian homes where Mom and Dad are committed to each other. Joe surveyed more than one thousand of these kids and found some encouraging things:

- Ninety-five percent of the boys say their fathers regularly tell them, "I love you."

- Ninety-eight percent of the girls say their mothers tell them regularly, "I'm proud of you" or "You're doing a great job."

- Ninety-one percent of the kids say their parents play games with them.

- Ninety-four percent say their fathers attend their athletic events.

- Ninety-seven percent of the boys say they get hugs from their dads.

- One hundred percent of the girls say they get hugs from their moms and dads.

- Recalling their childhood, 100 percent of the girls remember having stories read to them by their mothers. Eighty-five percent of the boys recall having stories read to them by their dads.

- Eighty-nine percent of the boys say their fathers have taken them fishing.

- One hundred percent of the girls say their parents have taken them to Sunday school.[5]

It's no coincidence that more than 80 percent of these kids say they are against premarital sex. It's no coincidence that 92 percent do not use illegal drugs. It's no coincidence that the majority of these kids don't drink alcohol.

Guys, let me ask you another question. If your kids go to off to camp one summer, and somebody asks them to fill out a survey, what are they going to say? Most of the kids at Joe's camp are not on the casualty list. Why not? It's quite simple, really. First, they were lucky enough to have a mom and dad that were committed to one another. Second, they had moms and dads that together invested in the lives of their kids. They invested by saying, "I love you." They invested by going to ball games, taking them fishing, playing assorted games, and handing out massive doses of hugs.

By the way, all of these things take time. Lots of time. You know the old debate about time, don't you? "Quality time" versus "quantity time." There are some well-meaning parents who realize that their careers take too much time from the family. So they empha- size "quality time." In their minds, their work is simply too demanding to have "quantity time." So they make sure the time they do have with their families is "qual- ity."

That sounds good. But it has one fatal error. *You never know when quality time is going to show up.* Quality time isn't the norm. Quality time is when you can talk heart to heart with your kids. Quality time is when your son asks you a serious question completely out of left field as you are trimming the bushes together. Quality time is when you're putting your daughter to bed at night, and she asks you to tell her a story about when you were a kid. And she will remember that story for the rest of her life.

Quality time comes at the most unusual moments. You never know when it will happen. It usually makes an appearance someplace in the realm of quantity time.

Tom Peters is a prolific writer on the subject of business and excellence. He has either authored or co-authored such best sellers as *In Search of Excellence, A Passion for Excellence*, and *Thriving On Chaos*. Listen to the words of this business guru who divides his time between his two homes in California and Vermont: "We are frequently asked if it possible to 'have it all'—a full and satisfying personal life and a full and satisfying, hard-working professional one. Our answer is: No. The price of excellence is time, energy, attention and focus, at the very same time that energy, attention and focus could have gone toward enjoying your daughter's soccer game. Excellence is a high cost item."[6]

High cost is right! It may cost you a child on the casualty list. It may cost you a child that turns to alcohol because Dad was never around. It may cost you a pregnant daughter who went to some adolescent male to meet her emotional needs because Dad was unavailable to fill her emotional tank.

Peters doesn't know it, but he's dispensing enemy propaganda. This successful writer is giving men permission to sacrifice their children on the altar of personal ambition. And he is wrong.

Peters is to be commended for his honesty, but his reasoning is barbaric. An expert in marketing, he is marketing Strategy #2. And ultimately, Strategy #2 will eat your lunch. The enemy will use anything to alienate you from your children. Even a "passion for excellence."

You know, I've got a passion to be an excellent father. And so do you. Otherwise you wouldn't have read this far. We need some men who have a passion to be better fathers than they are accountants. We need some men who have a passion to be better dads than they are attorneys, salesmen, foremen, pastors, or doctors.

Are you one of these men? You can be!

So far I've said two things: (1) War has been declared on the biblical family; (2) Satan has two specific goals in this war—to alienate you from your wife and to alienate you from your kids.

But I have something else I want to say.

Satan's Strategy in the War on the Family Is to Neutralize the Man

Leo Durocher was coaching first base in an exhibition game between the old New York Giants and the cadets at West Point. One noisy cadet kept shouting at Leo, doing his best to upset him. "Hey, Durocher," he hollered. "How did a little squirt like you get into the major leagues?" "My congressman appointed me," Leo shouted back.

That's how you got to be head of your family. You were appointed. Like it or not, you carry the responsibility. You are the point man.

The enemy is no fool. He has a strategically designed game plan, a diabolical method he employs time and time again. When he wants to destroy a family, he focuses on the man. For if he can neutralize the man . . . he has neutralized the family. And the damage that takes place when a man's family leadership is neutralized is beyond calculation.

Satan's approach is the same, whether he's doing combat in the church or in the family. If Satan can neutralize a pastor through financial impropriety or by a sexual escapade, he has neutralized that pastor's church as well. Not only the reputation of the pastor, but the reputation of the church has been tarnished. Satan's strategy has always been to neutralize the leaders. It works in the family, and it works in the church.

What that means is that we should *expect* to be attacked. We should *expect* extreme temptation to come our way. When you get serious about leading your family, you will be opposed.

If a man is passive and indifferent to the things of God and the spiritual leadership of his home, then attack is not necessary. He is already "neutralized."

But the moment a man gets serious about following hard after Christ, he can expect the shelling to start. The enemy wants you neutralized, and he is not pleased when you begin to give spiritual leadership to your wife and children.

May I ask a question? What do you suppose Jesus Christ thinks about the failure of men to assume their God-appointed leadership roles? Jesus Christ established the family. Jesus Christ was incarnated into a family. He had brothers, sisters, and a genealogy. Perhaps the Lord would look at our contemporary situation and modify something He said at another time, in another culture. Perhaps He would say something like this:

When He saw the fathers, He was filled with dismay, because so many quit, so many were set aside, and so many were plateaued and directionless. They had lost their zest for leading. They had no clear philosophy or direction for their leadership. They were leaderless leaders. Then He said to His disciples, "The harvest is plentiful, but the fathers with clear direction are few. Ask the Lord of the harvest, that He will send forth knowledgeable, discerning, and direction-oriented fathers into His harvest."[7]

In the war on the family, the harvest is our children. They are the leaders and the parents of the next generation.

What will turn the tide in the war on the family? In the months prior to the last presidential election, I heard many evangelicals talk about the necessity of electing a Christian president. "Wouldn't it be great to have a committed Christian in the White House?" they asked.

I would like to suggest something else that, in my opinion, would have far greater impact. If hundreds of thousands of men seriously began to lead their own homes, the impact on America would be far greater than one Christian man leading in the White House.

It is a scientific fact that when Canada geese fly in formation, they travel 70 percent faster than when they travel alone. If Christian men all over America would get into battle formation and begin to lead, we could turn this war around—and we could turn it quickly.

That's what I wanted to say.

Gentlemen, I know that you love your families. You love your wife. You love your children. You would be willing to die for them. In most wars, that's what men are asked to do. They go off to war because they're willing to die for their families.

But in this war, it's different. In this war, Jesus Christ is looking for men who will *live* for their families. That's what He would have you to do.

In the spiritual war on the family, it is father who leads best.

CHAPTER TWO

Save the Boys

*A boy is the only thing that
God can use to make a man.*

Cal Farley

A group of appreciative tourists watched a demonstration put on by the Royal Artillery of the Queen. The six-man team worked with flawless precision. Actually, only five of them worked with precision. One of the soldiers positioned himself about twenty-five yards away from the cannon and stood at attention during the entire exhibition, doing nothing.

After the exhibition, one of the tourists asked the staff officer to explain the duty of the man standing off to the side.

"He's number six," came the reply.

"Yes, but what does he do?"

"He stands at attention."

"Yes, I know, but *why* does he stand at attention?"

No one knew why number six stood at attention. None of the other five knew, the man himself didn't know, and even the commanding officer didn't know.

After many hours of research through old training manuals, it became clear what number six was to do. He was to hold the horses.

Why was number six standing at attention? Because he was appointed to do so. Did he have any idea what he was supposed to do? No.

I'm afraid there are too many husbands and fathers today who are in the same situation. When it comes to their families, they're simply standing there. Motionless. Like the sixth man in the Royal Artillery, they're making about as much difference in their homes as parsley on a plate of guacamole.

The sixth man had no idea he was supposed to be holding the horses. And too many men today have no idea that their job is to save the boys.

"If I could offer a single prescription for the survival of America, and particularly black America," writes William Raspberry, a black columnist with the *Washington Post,* "it would be restore the family. And if you asked me how to do it, my answer—doubtlessly oversimplified—would be: save the boys."[1]

Tragically, the black family in modern America has largely lost its boys. The enemy has effectively removed black males from their God-appointed positions of leadership and responsibility—and he has the same goal in mind for the rest of America. He may use different methods to achieve his goal, but his strategy is the same: Destroy the boys by neutralizing the males.

In a recent Bill Moyers television special on the black family, a teenage male who had fathered six children was asked about his responsibilities to the various mothers. His careless reply: "Ain't no woman gonna mess up my life."[2] As a result of this selfish mentality, we have an epidemic on our hands. Black boys grow up without male role-models and so have no one to emulate when they become adults.

Don Lewis, director of the Nehemiah Project, in testimony before the United States House of Representatives, summarized the crisis:

> Through decades of social policy . . . the federal government has gutted and plundered the black community of its husbands and fathers. The result is that boys learn that drugs and larceny are the fastest ways of making lots of cash. They simply don't have fathers who can teach and demonstrate the virtues of a healthy work ethic, the importance of sexual discipline and responsibility, the benefits of education and the beauty of transcendent values.[3]

So the cycle repeats itself, generation after generation.

Richard John Neuhaus puts it right on the table: "Millions of children do not know, and will never know, what it means to have a father. More poignantly, they do not know anyone who has a father or is a father . . . It takes little imagination to begin to understand the intergenerational consequences of this situation. It is reasonable to ask whether, in all of human history, we have an instance of a large population in which the institution of the family simply disappeared. It is reasonable and ominous, for the answer is almost certainly no. There is no historical precedent supporting the hope that the family, once it has disappeared, can be reconstituted."[4]

No, Raspberry did not oversimplify the solution. We must save the boys. I must save my boys, and you must save yours. If you don't have boys, then your energy should go into saving your girls. I know, because I have a very special daughter. Little boys and little girls must both be saved if the family in the next generation is going to have any kind of fighting chance. So whether it's all boys in your home, or all girls, or a mixture of both, it's our job to provide a model that will equip them to confidently take on the responsibilities of life and marriage. Our children are going to need godly spouses with whom they can raise the next generation for Christ.

If our boys are not equipped to lead families, then the families of the next generation will not have leaders. And neither will the next, for it becomes a vicious epidemic that multiplies with each successive generation.

Black America is in crisis because men abandoned their God-appointed roles. Today, the rest of America is on the same track, racing like a bullet-train to the same inevitable destination.

The Eternal Plan for Saving the Boys

From eternity, God instituted a divine plan for the family. It was to be followed by each generation. For thousands of years, it *was* followed. Phon Hudkins writes: "The family is the only social institution that is present in every single village, tribe, or nation we know through history. It has a genetic base and is the rearing device for our species."[5]

Note Hudkins's phrase "the rearing device for our species." God's plan has always been for families to raise children. But to raise them for what purpose? So that they may become competent and qualified to raise their own children! In other words, children learn from their parents' example how to raise the next generation.

But what happens when the chain is broken? What happens when a man abandons his wife and children and leaves them to fend for themselves? In particular, how is a boy to learn what it is to be a man when there is no man around to learn from?

Dave Simmons, who trains fathers all over the country in his excellent "Dad, the Family Shepherd" seminars, comments:

> "Plan A" for training family shepherds is the original, God-designed plan that calls for on-site, hands-on training in a master/apprentice relationship. It is a decentralized program with an instructor/student ratio of 1:2, 1:3, or 1:4 and takes anywhere from sixteen to twenty-two years. It is the father/son training program. Fathers are supposed to equip boys to become effective family shepherds. The task of a father is not to raise children: it is to equip child-raisers.[6]

Satan's strategy to counteract God's plan is a shrewd one. He simply focuses on luring a man away from his God-given responsibilities. So instead of being a committed to one woman in a marriage relationship, the man gives in to the temptation of bedding as many different women as possible. This model of "manliness" then becomes the pattern for the next generation of boys.

This is why we now have a situation "where millions of children do not know, and will never know, what it means to have a father. More poignantly, they do not know anyone who has a father or is a father."

Read that last sentence again, slowly. It staggers the imagination. We have a crisis on our hands without precedent. I'm an optimist, but the magnitude of this catastrophe overwhelms my ability to comprehend.

Perhaps it would be helpful if we could go back and observe God's original plan in action. Did you see the movie *Back to the Future*? If you did, you remember that Michael J. Fox got into a wild time machine (a souped-up DeLorean) and went back to the 1950s. Let's use our imaginations, get into our own DeLoreans, and go to back to the days when Rome ruled the world. Specifically, let's go back to the time when Jesus was being raised by Joseph and Mary.

Stephen Clark, in his monumental book *Man and Woman In Christ*, describes the normal Jewish family pattern in the days of Jesus: "In Jewish society . . . the mother had primary charge of all the children from their birth until approximately five to seven years of age. *At that time care of the boys would pass from the mother to the father* . . . This meant that he would live his life with his father. He would work along with his father, helping him and thereby gradually learning farming or his father's trade. During that time the father would form his son as a man. He would raise his son in his own presence and teach him all that he knew. In fact, much of the son's training would consist of his father's example. The son would see what the father was doing, and would thus learn what the father knew . . . his father was expected to equip him to function as an adult male."[7]

For literally thousands of years, this is how men functioned. Men raised their boys and as a result there was tremendous stability in the family. Men did not have identity crises. They knew who they were and what they were supposed to do because they had seen a model. Boys were specifically trained by their father's example to one day function as a father. It is hard for us to grasp here in the 1990s that this was the normal pattern for family life.

So what happened? Something obviously changed. Men don't raise their sons like that anymore. Why not? What was responsible for changing such a solid family structure that had endured for generation after generation?

The answer comes in three words: The Industrial Revolution. Not the sexual revolution, or the Revolutionary War, but the good old Industrial Revolution that we studied back in fourth grade. It's been awhile for most of us since we reviewed our fourth-grade notes on the Industrial Revolution, so let's get back in the DeLorean and head for 1750 A.D.

I recently spent an interesting hour or so flipping through our family's *World Book Encyclopedia*. I found some fascinating information:

> In 1750, farming was the most important occupation of all people. The ordinary man was a farmer and lived in a village. He

raised his own food, and unless he was near a large town he grew little more than he needed. Cloth and clothing, furniture, and tools and implements were made at home from wool, wood, and leather produced on the farm. The ordinary man bought little outside his village except iron for his plow point, salt, and perhaps an occasional ornament or bit of ribbon.

In the towns, which were generally quite small, some manufacturing was carried on. Such things as hardware, cloth, jewelry, silverware, swords, guns, cannons, and ammunition were produced by craftsmen working in their own shops with simple tools.[8]

Notice how life was built around the home prior to the Industrial Revolution. Four out of five Americans were farmers. Men worked at home, women worked at home, and so did the children. Their jobs were different, but everyone worked. The pattern remained the same as it had for centuries. The mother raised the children until they were somewhere between five and seven, then the boys would work with their fathers and the girls would work next to their mothers.

What about the one in five who weren't farmers? They were the silversmiths, blacksmiths, other types of "smiths," and various merchants. The same basic pattern applied to them. When a boy reached seven, he would go to work with his dad and learn his trade: blacksmith, gunsmith, or shoemaker. Most of the time, going to work simply meant going from one room to another: "in many cases, [they] used their front rooms as workshops and salesrooms, and lived in the back rooms."[9]

The point is clear. Prior to the Industrial Revolution, the normal pattern was for fathers to raise their sons. They were together nearly every waking hour. But this continuous style of family life was soon to change. In fact, it was already undergoing transition. As early as 1642, "Massachusetts united its various town schools into a system, and made it unlawful for parents to keep their children out of school."[10] Forces were already at work to minimize the time that children had with their parents. Up until this time, children's education came primarily through the tutelage of their parents.

As the Industrial Revolution began to take hold, more and more factories popped up. Until this time, a man's work had been done in the context of his home. Now employment became dependent upon these innovative factories.

"Here the workers were brought together to operate the machines . . . the ordinary worker could no longer expect to become an independent producer. He was reduced to the status of a factory hand. Factories tended to crowd together in city areas where coal and labor were cheap. Factory towns grew rapidly, and serious social evils developed."[11]

Doesn't that last sentence just drip with understatement? "Serious social evils developed." Why? Because the pattern of family life known for thousands of years was changing. The Industrial Revolution, which allowed people to enjoy more conveniences in life, was also responsible for rearranging the very structure of family life. And "serious social evils developed."

Weldon Hardenbrook explains what happened: "This dramatic transition literally jolted the role of men in America. Once farmers, and the children of farmers, these men exchanged work around their homes and families for new occupations in factories. And in most cases, this new situation required men to leave their homes for long periods of time."[12]

There is your answer as to why serious social evils developed. When factories became the source of income, men had to leave home, thus greatly diminishing their ability to influence their sons.

The formula is simple:

LESS TIME = LESS INFLUENCE.

It became increasingly harder to save the boys. Almost overnight, men stopped doing what they had done for thousands of years. They unknowingly brought to a halt the accumulated momentum of generations. Work now separated father from son, when for generations they had worked together in the master/apprentice relationship. Men stopped raising their boys because they weren't present to lead their boys. And as the years have gone by, that all-important male role model has eroded even further.

So it was over two hundred years ago that the seeds were planted which removed men from their God-appointed role of raising boys. In our generation, those seeds are bearing fruit. And the fruit is killing us.

The Influence of a Father

How does a boy learn what it is to be a man?

Harvard psychologist Samuel Osherson writes: "What does it mean to be male? If father is not there to provide a confident, rich model of manhood, then the boy is left in a vulnerable position . . . this situation places great pressure on the growing son . . . we often misidentify with our fathers, crippling our identities as men."[13]

We save our boys by giving them a role model to follow. When our boys have a clear role model, they intuitively know how to function when they assume the responsibility of marriage and parenting. But in this generation, there are too many crippled boys who have no idea what it is to be a man.

It is my God-appointed task to ensure that my sons will be ready to lead a family. I must equip them to that end. Little boys are the hope of the next generation. They are the fathers of tomorrow. They must know who they are and what they are to do. They must see their role model in action. That's how they will know what it means to be a male. That puts the ball in my court . . . and in yours.

I have three children. At this writing, Rachel is ten, John is eight, and Joshua is five. Rachel's primary role model is her mother. Generally speaking, the girls emulate their mother and the boys follow after dad. Guys, let's face it! Most of our wives are doing excellent jobs in getting our daughters ready for adulthood. Later in this book, I will deal specifically with a man's responsibility to his daughter. But for right now, I am going to assume your wife is carrying out her responsibility well in training your daughter.

This is a book for men. It's our job to save the boys. So the question is, how are we going to do that? My boys are eight and five. I've got ten years left with John before he heads out to college, thirteen with Josh. That time is simply going to fly by. So I must have a pretty clear idea of what I need to teach them during those remaining years. I must ask myself: *What do I specifically need to do in order to train them to become leaders of their families?*

I have five goals for saving my boys. It is my job as their father to model for them the importance of

- knowing and obeying Jesus Christ,
- knowing and displaying godly character,
- knowing and loving my wife,
- knowing and loving my children, and
- knowing my gifts and abilities, so I can work hard and effectively in an area of strength, rather than weakness, and contribute effectively to the lives of others—and have a little fun at the same time.[14]

A Primary Principle of Fathering

Dave Simmons is right on target when he says that error increases with distance. In my estimation, that's the primary principle of fathering. If you are going to save the boys, you have to be there.

I am an excellent bowler. I carry an average of 285. The goal of any bowler is a 300 game. Over the years, I have rolled nearly twenty 300 games.

But there's something I should mention. The length of a bowling alley is approximately sixty feet. I, however, prefer to bowl from about fifteen feet. When I bowl from fifteen feet, I enjoy the game a lot more. The majority of my balls are strikes, and when I do leave a spare, I always make it.

I'm dynamite from fifteen feet. But when I move back to the regulation line, my average drops dramatically. The reason is simple: Error increases with distance.

What is true in bowling is true in fathering. Error increases with distance. In other words, if I am going to be the family leader that God has called me to be, then I must BE THERE. On site. Consistently.

There are two ways that I must "be there." First, I must be there physically. This is where we have a real disadvantage compared to pre-Industrial Revolution generations. We get up in the morning and leave for work. Our kids get up and go to school, and we probably won't see them until dinner. We've lost a significant amount of time with our sons because the demands of our culture have taken the time away.

That means Christian men must realize the necessity of their being present *in the home.* When you deduct commute and work time from our waking hours, at best we have only two or three hours that can be used for being "with" one another. That time must be used wisely if we are going to influence our children. One man who didn't use the time wisely tells his story:

> I remember talking to my friend a number of years ago about our children. Mine were 5 and 7 then, just the ages when their daddy means everything to them. I wished that I could have spent more time with my kids but I was too busy working. After all, I wanted to give them all the things I never had when I was growing up.
>
> I love the idea of coming home and having them sit on my lap and tell me about their day. Unfortunately, most days I came home

so late that I was only able to kiss them good night after they had gone to sleep.

It is amazing how fast kids grow. Before I knew it, they were 9 and 11. I missed seeing them in school plays. Everyone said they were terrific, but the plays always seemed to go on when I was traveling for business or tied up in a special conference. The kids never complained, but I could see the disappointment in their eyes.

I kept promising that I would have more time "next year." But the higher up the corporate ladder I climbed, the less time there seemed to be.

Suddenly they were no longer 9 and 11. They were 14 and 16. Teenagers. I didn't see my daughter the night she went out on her first date or my son's championship basketball game. Mom made excuses and I managed to telephone and talk to them before they left the house. I could hear the disappointment in their voices, but I explained the best I could.

Don't ask where the years have gone. Those little kids are 19 and 21 now and in college. I can't believe it. My job is less demanding and I finally have time for them. But they have their own interests and there is no time for me. To be perfectly honest, I'm a little hurt.[15]

He's hurt? How do you think his kids felt growing up? Gentlemen, the point is this. We have a limited amount of time with our children. How much time do you have left?

Emotional Distance

Saving the boys requires more than just our physical presence. Even when the father is physically present in the home, the great danger is that he will be emotionally distant. This kind of father can emotionally cripple a boy for life.

James Carroll has said that the "curse of fatherhood is distance, and the good fathers spend their lives trying to overcome it."[16] Distance is just not physical, it is emotional. To save our boys, we must be there emotionally. We must be in tune with what is going on with our kids.

I am forty years old. It is my conviction that many men of my generation had fathers who were present physically but absent emotionally. The research bears this out.

Samuel Osherson did a study of 370 men who graduated from Harvard in the mid-1960s. These men are the "successes" of our society, the guys who made it. Armed with degrees from Harvard, they went out into their respective vocational battlefields and won . . . and won big. Yet many of them were scarred and wounded by fathers who were not there emotionally for them as they were growing up.

Osherson sums up his research: "The interviews that I have had with men in their thirties and forties convince me that the psychological or physical absence of fathers from their families is one of the great underestimated tragedies of our times."[17]

Osherson is right. The absence of fathers in the lives of their children—either physically or psychologically—is devastating. As you look around, you begin to see evidence of the tragedy.

George Vaillant interviewed successful business-men, scientists, and scholars who reached the age of forty-seven. As these successful men looked back over their lives, it became apparent that "in more than ninety-five percent of the cases, fathers were either cited as negative examples or were mentioned as people who were not influences."[18]

Every one of those forty-seven-year-old men is a part of the walking wounded in the war on the family. How effective do you think they have been in raising their own children?

Another psychologist, Jack Sternbach, critiqued the father-son relationship in seventy-one of his clients. His findings: "Fathers were physically absent for 23 percent of the men; 29 percent had psychologi-cally absent fathers who were too busy with work, uninterested in their sons, or passive at home; 18 per-cent had psychologically absent fathers who were aus-tere, moralistic, and emotionally uninvolved; and 15 percent had fathers who were dangerous, frightening to their son, and seemingly out of control. Only 15 percent of Sternbach's cases showed evidence of fathers appropriately involved with their sons. . . ."[19]

We may have had fathers who were absent from us but we cannot pass that on to our children. We must put a new link in the chain, a positive to replace a negative. If you do that, your boys will never have to deal with the emotional wounds that you may carry. We must save our boys so that we can save the family.

Not long ago, three military recruiters accepted an invitation to address the senior class of a local high school. Graduation was only a few months away, and the principal wanted his two hundred young men to hear of the options available in the military.

The assembly was to be forty-five minutes in length. It was agreed that each recruiter would have fifteen minutes to make his pitch and then have another twenty minutes in the cafeteria to meet with interested boys. The Army recruiter went first and got so excited about his speech that he went over twenty minutes. The Navy recruiter, not to be outdone, stood up and also spoke for twenty minutes.

The Marine Corps recruiter, realizing that his fifteen-minute speech had been cut to two, walked up to the podium and spent the first sixty seconds in silence. Wordlessly, he gazed over the group of high school seniors. They knew he was sizing them up. After what seemed to be an eternity, the recruiter said, "I doubt whether there are two or three of you in this room who could cut it as marines. I want to see those three men as soon as this assembly is dismissed." He then turned on his heel and sat down. Predictably, he was mobbed by a herd of young men when he arrived in the cafeteria.

The Marine Corps is always on the lookout for a few good men. So is the Lord. As a matter of fact, He wants you. And with His help, you can make a difference in this war.

One man *can* make a difference. Churchill saved England. Lombardi turned the Packers from doormats into legends. Namath convinced the Jets they could win the Super Bowl. Iacocca turned Chrysler around. It happens all the time. One man can make a difference.

Jonathan Edwards was one man who made a difference. Born in 1703, he was perhaps the most brilliant mind America ever produced. A pastor, writer, and later, president of Princeton, he and his wife had eleven children. Of his known male descendants

- more than three hundred became pastors, missionaries, or theological professors;

- 120 were professors at various universities;

- 110 became attorneys;

- sixty were prominent authors;

- thirty were judges;

- fourteen served as presidents of universities and colleges;

- three served in the U.S. Congress; and

- one became vice-president of the United States.[20]

Jonathan Edwards made a difference because he saved his boys. And his boys saved their boys. And those boys grew up to save their boys. Generation after generation, the boys were saved. He was just one man, but he positively affected hundreds and even thousands of his descendants after his death.

Although Edwards was known for his daily regimen of thirteen hours in the study and despite his busy schedule of teaching, writing, and pastoring, he made it a habit to come home and spend one hour each day with his children.

Edwards was one of the great minds of history. Yet, this world-class scholar had his priorities right. He not only made sure he made it home for dinner, but he got in at least one hour of family time each night. It's my guess that Edwards made a difference in generation after generation because he understood his God-appointed role as husband and father.

If you get into your DeLorean and travel into the future, what would your legacy look like? Would there be a chain linking generation to generation with godly men who in turn produced more godly men? Or is it going to be generation after generation of confused leadership from men who have no clear-cut role model?

The destiny of those future generations is in your hands. The choices that you make with your family today will determine the quality of life in your family tree for generations to come. That's why one man can make a difference. And if you save your boys, it will be the greatest and most fulfilling task of your life.

The decade of the '60s was a time when a lot of young men rebelled against their fathers. Anarchy, dope, easy sex, and rebellion was in vogue on the college campus. As David Crosby, of Crosby, Stills, Nash and Young, recently said, "Anybody who says he clearly remembers the '60s obviously wasn't there."

Yet I know three men, now between the ages of thirty-six and forty, who made it through that era virtually unscathed. What is interesting is that each of them had a father who trained them in the essentials of life. They each had a strong male role model.

Each of these men was raised in a Christian home. When they went off to college, each of them maintained his faith in Jesus Christ. Instead of rebelling against their faith, they grew in it. It is more than coincidence that each of these three men had a father who was committed to Jesus Christ.

After graduation, in due time, each of them got married. Each man has now been married for at least thirteen years. It is safe to say that each of these men not only loves his wife, but likes her. They're not just in love, they're in like. In other words, they thoroughly enjoy their marriages. It's more than coincidence that each of these men had a father who was committed to his wife.

Each of these men and their wives have been favored with the gift of children and enjoy close, loving relationships with their kids. It is more than coincidence that each of these men enjoyed the same kind of relationship with their dad while growing up.

Each of these men have done well in their chosen professions. They each work in careers that maximize their particular strengths and skills. And they are having fun. Interestingly enough, each of them had a father who worked in a profession that he thoroughly enjoyed.

Oh, by the way. There's something I failed to mention. Each of these three men had the same father. I know—I'm one of the three. What Steve Farrar, Mike Farrar, and Jeff Farrar have in common is Jim Farrar. We are all products of his leadership.

None of us choose our families or our fathers. But thanks to God's grace in our lives, the three of us were given a dad who modeled masculinity and leadership. He wasn't perfect. He'll tell you that. He tends to be irritable and impatient when he's tired (that's where we got it).

But he was very consistent, and each of us grew up to emulate his example. He married a lovely woman named Beverly, so each of us married lovely women named Beverly (well, we each found a lovely woman, but they wouldn't go for the name change).

He showed us what it meant to be a man. A genuine Christian man. A man who loves Jesus Christ, his wife, and his kids. He showed us *how* to do it. And humanly speaking, he is the one who is responsible for the quality of our lives today.

That's what the rest of this book is about. It's about *how* to be a male role model. Perhaps you haven't had the role model that gave you a clear idea of what you are to be as a husband or father. As a result, you don't have the confidence you'd like to have in your role as family leader.

Let me make you a promise. This book will help you fill in the blanks on what it means to lead a family. With the help of the Holy Spirit, you will be better equipped to save your boys.

One man can make a difference. Just as in the case of Mike, Jeff, or me. We know first-hand the difference one man can make.

As far as I know, my dad never planned on writing a book to men about saving their boys. He's a real estate broker and has been for more than forty years. Writing books is not his thing. But you should know something. He's the real author of this book. I just watched him and wrote it all down.

CHAPTER THREE

Real Men Don't

*The hand that means to make another clean,
must not itself be dirty.*
Gregory

Do you remember the book *Real Men Don't Eat Quiche*? It had some great one-liners on the definitive characteristics of a real man:

- Real men don't floss;
- Real men don't buy flight insurance;
- Real men don't play frisbee;
- Real men don't use zip codes;
- Real men don't call for a fair catch.

As I recall, there was also a light bulb joke going around about real men. Do you know how many real men it takes to change a light bulb? None. Real men aren't afraid of the dark.

I'd like to add a couple more one-liners. But these aren't funny. They're critically important to the survival of the family. Real men save their boys. And I can think of one thing in particular that real men must *not* do if they want to have any hope at all of saving their sons: Real men don't commit adultery.

An epidemic of staggering proportions is taking place in America. I'm not thinking of AIDS. I'm thinking of adultery. It's an epidemic that for the most part used to afflict only those outside of the body of Christ. No longer. This epidemic has not only found its way inside the church, but has wormed its way up to the highest echelons of church leadership.

There's something strange about this epidemic other than its rolling virtually unchecked through the body of Christ. What is strange is that we don't *call* it "adultery."

Richard Saul Wurman gets to the heart of the matter:

> Doublespeak is one the biggest problems in the English language, according to a National Council of Teachers state-of-the-language report. They cited the following examples: One stockbroker called the October 1987 stock market crash a "fourth-quarter equity retreat." The Pacific Gas and Electric Company referred to its bills as "energy documents." The shutdown at the General Motors plant in Framingham,

Massachusetts was labeled by the company as a "volume-related production-schedule adjustment." A recent publication claimed that jumping off a building could lead to "sudden deceleration trauma."[1]

Let's cut the doubletalk. Let's put the cards on the table. Let's call adultery what it is. In the war on the family, adultery is treason. But we don't call it treason. We have developed a more refined and sophisticated term. Adultery has become an "affair."

When a man leaves his wife and children for another woman and acts as impulsively as an aroused junior high kid on his first date, it's not an "affair." It's adultery. As George Bush would say, read my lips.

An affair . . .

That word has sort of a nice, light, airy ring to it. Like quiche. It certainly isn't a judgmental term like adultery. The word affair is fluffy and non-threatening. Affair is to adultery what quiche is to pot roast.

When I was a kid, I used to go to a fair. We would have a great time eating cotton candy, riding the ferris wheel, and playing games on the arcade. When you went to a fair, you left all the responsibilities of normal life behind, at least for a few hours. Life was a lot of fun at a fair.

Maybe that's why we call adultery an affair. It's leaving behind your responsibilities. But let me say something about real men that I failed to mention earlier. Real men don't have affairs because real men are responsible. Real men keep their commitments. Even when their personal needs are not being met the way that they would hope. Even when they are disappointed in their wives for some reason. And that is precisely the time when we need to be on our guard more than ever.

Let's track this word *affair* for a minute. Dennis Rainey has come up with the best definition of an affair that I know of. According to him, an affair is an escape from reality, or a search for meaning outside the marriage.[2]

Ponder that definition for a minute. Think of the people you know personally who have been involved in an affair. Does that describe their motivation? It probably does.

In the last several years we have seen numerous Christian leaders exposed for their affairs. It seems like hardly a month goes by that I don't hear of some pastor or ministry leader who has succumbed to the lure of an affair. No wonder we have a credibility crisis in Christianity.

Warren Wiersbe tells of the great artist Raphael, who was painting his famous Vatican frescoes when a couple of bureaucratic churchmen stopped by to watch and criticize.

"The face of the apostle Paul is too red," said one.

"He blushes to see into whose hands the church has fallen," replied Raphael.[3]

Alexis de Tocqueville, who visited and wrote about America in the last century, said, "I sought for the greatness and genius of America in her commodious harbors and her ample rivers, and it was not there; in her fertile lands and boundless prairies, and it was not there. Not until I went to the churches of America and heard her pulpits aflame with righteousness did I understand the secret of her genius and power.

America is great because she is good, and if America ceases to be good, America will cease to be great."[4]

In our day, America has obviously chosen not to be good. Abortion on demand, the hysterical cry for homosexual rights, and laws that protect child pornographers are proof of that. But the righteousness and goodness that de Tocqueville described is not optional for the body of Christ.

We have seen too many in recent years who have preached righteousness in the pulpit while practicing unrighteousness in some hotel room. We have seen too many who have publicly advocated righteousness with tremendous fervor but have privately practiced immorality with even greater intensity.

Righteousness must not only be found in our pulpits, but in our homes. The home is the church in miniature, and every Christian father has been appointed pastor of his own home. Christian men, whether they are leading in the church or in their home, must seek after righteousness.

We all shake our heads when preachers proclaim one thing in public but do another in private. But adulterous acts aren't restricted just to those in full-time ministry. Those men just get more publicity. In this war, Christian men of all vocations are going down. Men who started well, men who were at one time committed to Jesus Christ and their families, walked into an ambush and so destroyed their credibility and integrity. Enticed to pursue an affair, they now live every moment with the consequences of their treasonous act.

How do Christian men get pulled into adultery? And how can we protect ourselves from having the same tragedy happen to us? Scripture gives the antidote when it says, "Be very careful, then, how you live—not as unwise but as *wise*" (Ephesians 5:15).

Do you remember the old hymn "Rise Up, O Men of God"? Someone ought to write a new one titled "Wise Up, O Men of God." Whether you are a CPA, pastor, attorney, or a salesman, an affair starts the same way. If we are to avoid the quicksand, we must wise up to the schemes of the enemy.

It usually begins with discontent. Things have changed. It's not the way it used to be between the two of you. You may have no explanation for it. Things are just . . . different.

You don't seem to have the same good times you had when you were dating. You rarely enjoy good conversation. You're just not close. You eat at the same table, share the same bathroom, sleep in the same bed, but you might as well be hundreds of miles apart.

If there's one word that describes your marriage, it's "distance." There remains little sense of sharing anything in your lives. You simply co-exist. The thrill is gone. Your marriage isn't just predictable, it's boring. And you are disappointed.

If there is a lack of sexual fulfillment, the frustration is especially acute—and a man who is not fulfilled sexually is especially vulnerable to outside temptation. Yet the sexual relationship is simply a reflection of the overall state of the marriage.

Remember the definition? An affair is an escape from reality or a search for fulfillment outside marriage. Now, let's construct a typical scenario for an affair to take place in the life of a man who is either bored or frustrated with his marriage.

Perhaps you had never noticed her. But as you walked by her desk today, she looked up and smiled. Or maybe she's the new receptionist for a client you've been calling on for several years. Or perhaps a new project involves two different departments working together, and suddenly you're spending large amounts of time with a woman you didn't even know two weeks ago. Or maybe she's in the church and has come to you for counsel.

Whatever the reason or the circumstances, you now find yourself relating to another woman. She's attractive and a lot of fun to be around. She always looks like a million bucks. If you were single, you would definitely ask her out.

This is how an affair gets started. You're frustrated and disappointed with your wife. Your needs aren't being met. And then *she* comes along.

Here's where it gets tricky. It is what you do in these innocent situations that will either make you or break you. If you don't make the right choices here, within a matter of weeks or even days you are going to get emotionally hooked. And once you've swallowed a hook, it's almost impossible to spit it out.

The central issue here is how to avoid taking the hook. Most men don't realize how vulnerable they are in these situations. Every marriage has its "down" times, and if a man doesn't recognize his increased vulnerability during these phases, he is sure to get himself in the deep weeds.

Randy Alcorn suggests that you ask some important questions to determine if there is a hook lodged in your emotional jaw.

- Do I look forward in a special way to my appointments with this person?

- Do I seek to meet with her away from the office in a more casual environment?

- Do I prefer that my co-workers not know I'm meeting with her again?[5]

If the answer to any of these questions is yes, then a red light should be going off on your dashboard. What do you do if you find yourself in this kind of situation?

In battle, it is called "retreat."

Remember Paul's instruction in 1 Corinthians 6:18? The *modus operandi* here is to flee immorality. That means back off, Jack. That means you stop having lunch with her. If you work together, then so be it. But don't do anything else than work. Stop taking side trips to go by her desk. She is Off-limits, with a capital "O."

Let me point out something I've discovered in talking with men who find themselves in this type of scenario. Up until now, absolutely nothing has happened. *What's the harm?* they ask themselves. *We're just talking.* That is precisely the harm. Ninety-nine men out of a hundred don't realize they are being set up by the enemy.

The problem with getting together and talking is this: The woman will be interested in what you have to say. As you discuss your ideas and plans, you will undoubtedly find her to be encouraging. You will begin to sense an attitude of understanding and appreciation that perhaps you haven't gotten at home recently.

Whether you mean to or not, you will begin to compare her with your wife, and your wife is going to lose. Why will your wife lose? Because if there are needs in your life that your wife is not currently meeting, and this woman has a great deal of respect and interest in you, your wife can't help but come in second.

If you and your wife are struggling, this woman probably will be more understanding than your wife. But why is she more understanding? I hate to be the one who breaks the news, but it's probably because she doesn't know you very well. All she sees are your strong points. Especially since you are working overtime to impress her. If she knew you as well as your wife does, would she be so understanding? I doubt it.

If a man saw clearly at this point, he would realize that he is living in an unreal world. That, remember, is the definition of an affair. It is an escape from reality or a search for fulfillment outside marriage. The attraction is simply this: You are tired of fighting the battle at home, and with this new companion there is no battle. That is the temptation. But look out, friend. You're about to step on a land mine.

Do you see how subtle the enemy is? If some attractive woman were to walk into your office at 3:30 P.M., remove her clothes, and say, "Let's get physical!" you would call for security. That approach is too blatant. It repels rather than attracts. So the enemy doesn't use it.

But he constantly uses the approach we are discussing. He uses it for the same reason USC used to run O.J. Simpson countless times during a game. It works. It works with bankers, stockbrokers, real estate agents, research technicians, and pastors. An enormous number of men have fallen through this subtle and seemingly harmless process.

What does a guy do when he wakes up and realizes he's on the verge of becoming emotionally hooked with another woman? I've talked with a number of men who have suddenly realized the implications of their emotional relationship. It has gone no further than an emotional attraction. No physical moves have been made. But it's decision time.

The choice at this point is to go one of two ways. The first is to realize that you are in almost over your head. You are in a very dangerous situation. You did not realize you were standing so close to the edge of the cliff. Suddenly, it is clear. The decision must be made to back off, to nip this thing in the bud before it goes any further. And the decision must be made and acted upon immediately. That is the rational and wise response.

The second response reveals a guy who is already emotionally hooked. It's called rationalization. When a guy says, "Hey, it's no big deal. We're just having lunch. I can handle it," then he has already taken the bait . . . hook, line, and sinker.

Boake Carter once said that "in time of war, the first casualty is truth." Don't flatter yourself. You *can't* handle it. You are lying to your soul.

Alcorn writes that "a relationship can be sexual long before it becomes erotic. Just because I'm not touching a woman, or just because I'm not envisioning specific erotic encounters, does not mean I'm not becoming sexually involved with her. The erotic is usually not the beginning but the culmination of sexual attraction."[6]

Maybe at this point you've got the feeling that someone has been reading your mail . . . because this is the kind of situation you're involved in right now. If that is true, you should know that you are not alone. My guess is that there are hundreds of Christian men, if not thousands, who are either currently in this situation or soon will be.

Why do I say that? Because it is the primary approach the enemy uses to lure a man away from his marriage. He does it in such a subtle and innocuous way that most guys never realize they are on their way to becoming dead meat. Proverbs 7:21-23 puts it this way:

> With persuasive words she led him astray;
> she seduced him with her smooth talk.
> All at once he followed her
> like an ox going to the slaughter,
> like a deer stepping into a noose
> till an arrow pierces his liver,
> like a bird darting into a snare,
> little knowing it will cost him his life.

I remember a lunch I had with a guy several years ago. He was married, in his late thirties, and had a couple of kids. He was an executive with a large ministry organization. He had been in the business world for a number of years and had recently taken a huge cut in pay to work for this Christian venture. He appeared to be a committed Christian with a sharp family.

As we were talking, I mentioned a book that I had just finished reading on marriage. He lit up. "I've been studying that book with a friend for the past six months, and it has helped both of our marriages," he said enthusiastically.

For the next ten minutes, he told me what he had been learning in the study with his friend. "Yes," he said in summary, "I would recommend that book to anyone. It has helped me grow closer to my wife and my friend to grow closer to her husband."

Suddenly, a blip appeared on my radar screen. Did he say it helped his friend grow closer to *her husband?* For some reason, I had been assuming (and I think it was a fair assumption) that the "friend" was a he.

I have a sophisticated approach to counseling. Basically, if I find a scab, I pick it until it bleeds. I had definitely found a scab. So I picked.

I began to ask him some general questions about his marriage. Then I asked him about his friend. He made it clear she was a strong Christian and that their relationship was strictly platonic. But the more I probed, the more he backtracked. After several minutes, I thought it was time to be direct.

Whenever I want to ask someone a real personal question I usually say, "Can I have your permission to ask you a personal question?" For some reason, people almost always say yes. He said yes, too. So I asked him a personal question.

"Why are you studying that book on marriage with someone else's wife?" I asked. "Have you ever thought of studying it with *your* wife?"

I should have guessed what was coming. "My wife doesn't understand me," came the reply.

"But your friend does understand you, right?"

"Yes, we can really communicate."

"May I ask you another pointed question?"

"Sure."

"Are you involved with your friend physically?"

"Of course not," he shot back.

"Have you ever hugged her?" He didn't say anything.

"Have you kissed her yet?" No reply.

"Can I take a guess who your friend is?"

"Oh, you don't know her."

"When I came into the office, there was a pretty blond receptionist. Tall, late twenties, very outgoing. Is that your friend?"

He didn't say anything, he just gazed out the window like a man looking for a bus that was an hour late.

I had already pressed my luck, so one more wasn't going to hurt. "I'm not a prophet, but let me make a prediction. Within six months, you'll be in bed together."

He nearly came out of his chair. "That will never happen!"

"Sure it will. I may be off on the time, but it'll happen."

This guy was mad now. "That-will-never-happen," he swore through clinched teeth.

As kindly as I could, I told him the reason that it would happen was that he was convinced it *couldn't* happen. And pride always comes before the fall.

It could happen to me. It could happen to you. It has happened to my friends. It has happened to yours. Better men than us have gone down. None of us are exempt. We are in spiritual warfare and given the wrong circumstances, any one of us could go down at any time.

We are in the greatest danger of all when we think we are safe. When a guy begins to think that this could never happen to him, then he needs to think again. I once heard Joe Aldrich, president of Multnomah School of the Bible, make a statement that sent a literal chill down my spine. Aldrich said, "Have you ever noticed how many men in the Bible failed in the second half of life? Our enemy is so cunning that he will wait forty or even fifty years to set a trap." That's precisely what happened to King David.

That's why we can never deceive ourselves into thinking we are somehow "above" sexual sin. The moment you begin to view yourself in that light, you can be sure that your carcass will one day be hanging in cold storage.

I came on pretty strong with this guy. He was so far gone on this woman that my only hope of pulling him back was to hit him hard. He knew the Scriptures, and he knew in his heart of hearts that he was wrong. But it was too late. He had taken the hook. He was already dead meat. Within weeks he walked out on his family.

Another discarded wife. Two more shattered children. Another family for the casualty list. Why? Because he bought the lie that the grass is always greener on the other side of the fence. But it never is.

The problem is simply this: When you leave your wife to commit adultery with another woman, you take yourself with you. And you are your biggest problem. I am my biggest problem, and you are yours. You are walking into this new relationship with the same personality, strengths, and weaknesses you have in your current marriage. And if you can't work out things with your current wife, what makes you think it will be any different with another woman? You are a major part of the problem, and unfortunately, you must take yourself along with you.

Undoubtedly, some of you reading this are thinking, "Hey, wait a minute! This all sounds great, but you don't understand my situation. I'm absolutely miserable. I'd be better off in prison than in this marriage. In fact, that's exactly how I feel. I'm in prison because [insert applicable reason here]:

> . . . my wife has refused to have sex with me for the past two years;

> . . . my wife has put on seventy-five pounds since our last child was born and although she used to be very attractive to me, I'm not physically attracted to her now at all;

> . . . my wife is my greatest critic—she doesn't support me or encourage me in any way. Her greatest pleasure in life is to put me down, especially in front of other people."

I know those kinds of situations are very real and painful. Let me give an abbreviated response here and recommend a book that speaks to this kind of hopeless situation. First of all, God knows your situation and understands it. He fully comprehends the extent of your misery. He understands the depth of your frustration.

Second, there is a tremendous phrase found in 1 Samuel 2:30 that has universal application to those who will live by it. In that verse, God gives a remarkably encouraging principle: "Those who honor me I will honor."

I do not want to minimize your prison of circumstances, but I do want to remind you that you are not the first of God's people to find themselves in prison. It may be a literal prison, a prison of leukemia, a prison of a wheelchair, or a prison of marriage. But if you will remain faithful, God will honor you. I believe that your misery can be replaced by joy as you remain faithful and trust God to honor your faithfulness.

I'm not suggesting there is an easy, overnight solution to your problem. But I am suggesting that divorce or adultery is not the solution it appears to be. Even those outside the evangelical camp will tell you that. As writer Pat Conroy observed upon his own marriage dissolution, "Each divorce is the death of a small civilization."

There is nothing wrong with desiring happiness, but horrendous problems develop when we become disobedient to obtain it. God rewards the obedient, and He is able to do far more than any of us could ever ask or think. He knows your situation. He has not forgotten you. And if you will remain faithful, you will see Him work on your behalf in ways you cannot fathom.

If you are on the freeway looking for true happiness, do not take the exit marked "adultery." It may look like a shortcut but it isn't. It's a dead end. Keep driving until you find the exit marked "obedience." That's the only road that will get you to genuine happiness.

What you are looking for cannot be found outside of God's will. It is clearly not His will that you violate your marriage covenant. Paul Kaufman tells the old story about two men from different villages. The first man dreams of great treasure buried in the other village. He travels to this village to find the treasure and there meets the second man who tells him that he too has had a strange dream about a treasure. You can guess where the second man dreamed the treasure was buried.

If you think you have misery now, wait until you commit adultery or get a divorce. You will regret it the rest of your life. When a man leaves his wife for an alliance with another woman, he is not only breaking God's commandment, he is making a decision that will only fuel and magnify his personal disappointment.

Donald W. McCullough accurately describes this counterfeit philosophy: "We think we know what will secure greater happiness—marriage or divorce, a higher salary or professional recognition, steamier sex or deeper intimacy, a new faith or better spiritual experiences—the list is as long as humans are ingenious in imagining greener grass on the far side of the fence. But we don't realize how hungry we really are. Small potatoes won't satisfy. We need a banquet table only God can spread."[7]

If you are in miserable circumstances as you read these words, you obviously feel as though you are stuck with the small potatoes. But if you will honor God by being obedient, He will honor you by throwing you some kind of banquet. I can't tell you how, I can't tell you when, but I can tell you that He keeps His word. He is the God of surprises, and if you remain faithful in that tough marriage, He will surprise you one day with joy.

Pat Williams, general manager of the Orlando Magic of the NBA, had a hopeless situation on his hands. Through his own neglect, his wife had become emotionally dead to him. But he determined that he would be faithful and do everything he could do to correct his mistakes. Could it be that one reason a wife gains excessive weight or incessantly criticizes a husband is that she doesn't feel secure in his love? Suffice it to say that Williams's book, *Rekindled*, tells how one man properly responded to God in a situation that looked hopeless. And God honored him for it. He will honor you as well.

The lure of adultery is that another woman will truly meet your needs. The lie of adultery is that no other woman on the face of the earth, no matter how alluring, interesting, or beautiful, has the capacity to fully meet the needs of another human being. That's why adultery is the ultimate hoax. It promises what it cannot deliver.

Real men protect themselves against adultery. Real men think seriously about the consequences of such an act. As they do, they ponder the facts, not the fantasies. They consider the long-range implications of having a fling. They count the cost. And that's why they don't do it—it just isn't worth it. If you don't believe that, ask someone who has done it. He will show you the broken shards of a shattered life. He will show you the pain and disappointment that comes from making a series of wrong choices.

Let me address the man who is currently involved in adultery. You know it's wrong, and you want to stop. So what do you do? There is only one solution and that is to take *extreme action*. Donald Joy is right: "Once a relationship has moved to genital contact, it will not be terminated so long as access to privacy remains."[8] In other words, you are going to have to bring in a trusted third party to help you break the relationship. The privacy and all the deceit must come to an end. If you continue to keep this sexual liaison private, you will never stop on your own.

You must go to your pastor, or to another mature, wise Christian you respect and trust who can give you clear, biblical steps to ending this destructive relationship. You must approach this confidant with complete honesty and a willingness to do whatever it takes to make things right.

You can be sure of one thing. If you don't take this step on your own, eventually your sin will find you out. This deception cannot go on indefinitely without someone finding out. I urge you to take the initiative. If you do, God will honor you for taking the hard step. If you don't, He will hound you as incessantly as He hounded David. David lived in deceit for a year before Nathan publicly confronted him (see chapters 11 and 12 of 2 Samuel). That was necessary because he refused to listen to the private voice of God in his heart. Don't make that mistake. Deal with it now.

Cultural Desensitization

I'm convinced that one of the reasons so many Christian guys go down is that we have become desensitized to the sin of adultery. It doesn't scare us. It doesn't shock us. We've become used to it. Adultery used to mean betrayal. Adultery used to jar and jolt our moral sensibilities. Now it only means that some guy was "trying to find himself." We describe it as a "momentary lapse of judgment."

Yet the fact of the matter is that adultery is an unspeakable act of betrayal. Adultery means that a man has sexual intercourse with a woman other than his wife. It means that they meet in some carefully chosen, romantic hotel and violate the clear commandment of God. As the lights are low and the commandment of God is even dimmer, he proceeds to kiss and caress a woman other than his wife. It's just a matter of minutes before they are naked together in bed. At this point, there is no turning back. They are naked and not ashamed—but they should be. Within a few steamy, passionate moments, he will insert his penis into her vagina.

I'm sure that last statement shocked you. Let me assure you that was my full intention. The act of adultery is shocking. But we have become so desensitized to it that we need to be shocked. You probably did not expect to read such a graphic description of the sexual act in a Christian book. You may have been offended that I used the terms penis and vagina. I assure you that I debated with myself for days about being so graphic.

I decided to include it because it proves the point. Most of us are more offended by the terms penis and vagina in a Christian book than we are by the term adultery. Adultery has lost its meaning. Sexual intercourse with another woman is a monstrous betrayal. But we hear about it at the office, we see it on TV, and absorb it at the movies. As a result, it has lost its bite. There's nothing to it anymore. We've compromised our standards, and as a result, adultery no longer offends us.

Adultery has even become acceptable for spiritual leaders. I'm convinced that one of the reasons we have an epidemic of adultery in the pulpit is that it no longer carries severe consequences. The reason that it does not include severe consequences is that we no longer consider it a severe act. When a gifted spiritual leader commits sexual sin, our greatest concern is how quickly he can be restored to ministry. Adultery used to mean that a man gave up the privilege of ministry. Now, with time off for good behavior, it means that after a year or so he may reenter the pulpit and continue to minister. Let's face it. Adultery has become acceptable behavior for leaders in the evangelical church.

It is no mistake that in the Old Testament God chose to put the mark of His covenant with Israel on the male penis. He didn't put it on the arm, or on the elbow, or on the thigh. God demanded that every Jewish man be circumcised on his sexual organ to remind him of the fact that he belonged to God.

Too many evangelical pulpits are filled by men who have slept with women other than their wives. How many are there? I don't know, but one would be too many. Is it any wonder we are not having a greater impact upon our culture for Christ?

Yes, there is forgiveness and grace to the one who has committed adultery. God offers pure forgiveness and grace to cover all our sins. We cannot afford ever to lose that principle. The church lost it for nearly fifteen hundred years until Martin Luther rediscovered it and brought about that historical earthquake that registered 9.0 on the Richter scale. That great earthquake is known as the Reformation.

Robert Farrar Capon gives a play-by-play description of what happened when grace was rediscovered:

"The Reformation was a time when men went blind, staggering drunk because they had discovered, in the dusty basement of late medievalism, a whole cellarful of fifteen-hundred-year-old, two-hundred proof grace—of bottle after bottle of pure distillate of Scripture, one sip of which would convince anyone that God saves us singlehandedly. The word of the Gospel—after all those centuries of trying to lift yourself into heaven by worrying about the perfection of your bootstraps—suddenly turned out to be a flat announcement that the saved were home free before they started. . . . Grace was to be drunk neat: no water, no ice, and certainly no ginger ale . . ."[9]

If you are reading this and adultery is in your past or in your present, know there is forgiveness available as you simply call upon the Lord with a repentant heart. But forgiveness is not the only issue in this dialogue about the epidemic of adultery . . . especially when it concerns a spiritual leader.

Forgiveness is available to all. But forgiveness does not automatically restore the privilege of leadership. Let me offer a critical principle: *In the New Testament, forgiveness is free, but leadership is earned.* It is earned by the power of a man's life. Sin, although forgiven, always sets off practical consequences. A mature, spiritual leader who sins and repents is forgiven, but he is not exempt from the series of aftershocks that will come his way from his disobedience.

I carefully chose the word "mature" in the previous sentence. A young man in his teens or early twenties is in the stages of developing character; that's why we normally don't put him in the upper levels of leadership. Several years ago, I had dinner with a group of men who all lead various ministries. The average age was somewhere around forty. As we ate, the conversation turned to our conversions and some of the foolish and wrong things we did as young believers in college. There was drunkenness, cheating in school, drugs, sexual immorality, bar brawls, and a few other activities (I was shocked to hear this since I have a completely spotless past. Ha!)

Let me hasten to add that the Lord disciplined every one of us as a father would discipline a young, immature son. God was disciplining us because He wanted to give every one of us spiritual responsibilities. But first we had to take some character examinations. If you don't pass on the first try, you'll take it again, and again, and again, until you do pass and God can entrust leadership into your hands. If you continue to fail these early tests of integrity, He never will entrust leadership to you.

I have a friend who came to Christ in his early twenties. He had lived a life of sexual promiscuity. For at least two years after his conversion, he continued to periodically sleep with women. His remorse and repentance were great. He came to grips with his sinful pattern and dealt with it head-on. Today, twenty years later, he is being used of God in a significant way. He is committed to his wife and has been sexually clean for nearly twenty years.

My point is this: All of us in our youthfulness did some pretty stupid things. I wouldn't think of driving a car at a speed of 105 miles per hour on the Bayshore Freeway south of San Francisco—especially on Friday at 7 P.M. But that's exactly what I did with two friends twenty-four years ago.

Billy Sunday once said that "a sinner can repent, but stupid is forever." That's a funny line, but we mustn't remain stupid forever. We expect people to grow up emotionally. We expect men over thirty to act differently than they did when they were under twenty.

That's why there is a difference between the sin of an immature believer and the sin of a mature one who is in leadership. And when a mature spiritual leader in the second half of his life commits sexual immorality, there are severe consequences. Please understand that I am not excusing sin at any age. I am saying, however, that those mature men who are in spiritual leadership are held to a higher standard. That's the crux of James 3:1: "Let not many of you become teachers, my brethren, knowing that as such we shall incur a stricter judgment" (NASB).

Chuck Swindoll hits the nail on the head. "Ministry is a character profession. To put it bluntly, you can sleep around and still be a good brain surgeon. You can cheat on your mate and have little trouble continuing to practice law. Apparently, it is no problem to stay in politics and plagiarize. You can be a successful salesperson and cheat on your income tax. But you cannot do those things as a Christian or as a minister and continue enjoying the Lord's blessing. You must do right in order to have true integrity. If you can't come to terms with evil or break habits that continue to bring reproach to the name of Christ, please, do the Lord (and us in ministry) a favor and resign."[10]

David was a real man, a man after God's own heart. But after committing adultery, he was never again quite the same. He was forgiven, but the aftershocks devastated his family. His adultery was a detestable act and God "set events in motion that would trouble David till his death."[11]

Some point out that David was allowed to keep his office of king even after his sexual sin. That's true. But in Israel, the king was not in "the ministry." He was a politician. The spiritual offices were prophet and priest. David didn't lose his office because he didn't have a spiritual office. But apparently he did lose his razor-sharp edge of credibility, and until his dying day he never completely got it back. One look at his family will underscore that.

A spiritual leader is to be a man above reproach (1 Timothy 3:2). Nelson Rockefeller once said, "My grandfather never broke any laws, but he did cause some new ones to be written." That cannot be said about those who are in spiritual leadership. They are to be above reproach. A Christian minister who has copulated with another woman does not fit the criteria. Sin has consequences, and for the man who once filled the pulpit, the pulpit is now off-limits. Tragically, he has lost the privilege that was once his.

Charles Haddon Spurgeon was the most influential preacher in England one hundred years ago. He was the Swindoll of his day. If he were around today, we would call him Chuck Spurgeon. His wise words are extremely relevant to our own day: "I hold very stern opinions with regard to Christian men who have fallen into gross sin. I rejoice that they may be truly converted, and may be mingled with hope and caution received into the church; but I question, gravely question whether a man who has grossly sinned should be very readily restored to the pulpit. As John Angell James remarks, 'When a preacher of righteousness has stood in the way of sinners, he should never again open his lips in the great congregation until his repentance is as notorious as his sin.' . . . My belief is that we should be *very slow* to help back to the pulpit men, who having once been tried, have proved themselves to have too little grace to stand the crucial test of ministerial life."[12]

Over two hundred years ago, Robert Murray McCheyne wrote to a young ministerial student who was abroad studying German: "I know you will apply hard to German, but do not forget the culture of the inner man—I mean of the heart. How diligently the cavalry officer keeps his sabre clean and sharp; every stain he rubs off with the greatest care. Remember you are God's sword, His instrument—I trust, a chosen vessel unto Him to bear His name. In great measure, according to the purity and perfection of the instrument, will be the success. It is not great talents God blesses so much as likeness to Jesus. A holy minister is an awful weapon in the hand of God."[13]

I realize that many of you reading this are not in full-time ministry. But if you are a Christian husband and father who is serious about leading his family, then you *are* in the ministry. The offices of husband and father are also character professions. And what McCheyne said about ministers is true of you as well. If a holy minister is an awful weapon in the hands of God, then so is a holy husband.

The moral compromises in our churches and homes have got to stop. We have given ourselves permission to seek the company of other women if our wives aren't meeting our needs. We have lowered the biblical standards of holiness because we have been inappropriately influenced by our culture. We are the salt, and we have lost our saltiness. If we ever hope to raise moral standards outside the church, then we had better begin by raising them within the church.

Mozart was once criticized by his patron, the emperor of Austria, for creating music that contained too many notes. The emperor suggested that a few of them could be cut. Mozart asked which few he had in mind.[14]

We live in a culture that thinks Ten Commandments are too many and which especially would like to cut the seventh. The seventh commandment clearly states, "You shall not commit adultery." Yet it is precisely the seventh commandment that holds families together.

I remember a number of years ago watching Phyllis George interview Dallas Cowboy superstar Roger Staubach. It was a typical, dull sort of interview until Phyllis blindsided the quarterback with this question: "Roger, how do you feel when you compare yourself with Joe Namath, who is so sexually active and has a different woman on his arm every time we see him?"

How would *you* reply in front of several million people?

We've all seen Staubach keep his cool in pressure game situations, and the tension in the air this time was just as great. But once again, Staubach kept his cool.

"Phyllis," he said calmly, "I'm sure I'm as sexually active as Joe. The difference is that all of mine is with one woman."

Touchdown! Roger hit the end zone with that comeback. Real men don't commit adultery. A real man sticks with one woman. Period.

CHAPTER FOUR

One-Woman Kind of Man

"It's not my fault when you consider that my three husbands have had twenty wives."

> Ava Gardner, on being asked about her failed marriages to Mickey Rooney, Artie Shaw, and Frank Sinatra

Hernando Cortés had a plan.

He wanted to lead an expedition into Mexico to capture its vast treasures. When he told the Spanish governor his strategy, the governor got so excited that he gave him eleven ships and seven hundred men. Little did the governor know that Cortés had failed to tell him the entire plan.

After months of travel, the eleven ships landed in Veracruz in the spring of 1519. As soon as the men unloaded the ships, Cortés instituted the rest of his plan. He burned the ships.

That's what you call commitment. That's what you call no turning back. That's what you call burning your bridges. Cortés didn't have any bridges. So he burned the ships.

By burning the ships, Cortés eliminated the options. He didn't know what he would encounter on his expeditions to the interior. He didn't know the strength of the people he would be fighting. But he did know this: There were now no escape routes for his men. If the fighting got too fierce, or the expedition got too exhausting, there would be no talk of going back to Veracruz and sailing home. In one fell swoop, he had not only eliminated their options but had created an intensely powerful motivation to succeed. Like it or not, they were now committed.

Gentlemen, if we are going to save the boys then we must save our marriages. And there is only one way to save our marriages. We have to burn our ships.

Burning your ships expresses commitment. Commitment is saying that no matter what comes in the future, you're going to stick it out. Commitment means that you have obligated yourself to follow through on your word. A commitment is your personal guarantee that you will do what you promised.

A number of years ago when I was pastoring, a man sat in my office. He was in his early sixties, had been married to the same woman for nearly forty years, and had five grown children and numerous grandchildren. He had been a committed Christian since coming to Christ in high school. For years, he had been a pillar in the evangelical community, serving as a leader in his church as well as on the boards of various Christian ministries. He had an excellent grasp of the Scriptures and had influenced hundreds of young people for Christ.

Why were we meeting? To discuss his teaching a Bible class for men? To look into the possibility of his mentoring some younger men in the church? No. We were meeting to discuss why he was involved in an immoral relationship for the past five years with a girl younger than his own daughters.

He didn't even try to deny his sin. A sharp thinker, he had developed a tight web of rationalizations that even included some scriptural references. As I continued to probe and slice through his web of excuses, finally, after about thirty minutes, he heaved a great sigh and blurted out, *"Don't I have a right to be happy?"*

In that one statement he captured the spirit of our age. We live in an era where commitment is cheap. It's cheap in marriage, business, politics, and even athletics. Commitment is cheap in professional sports when a running back will sign a six-year, multi-million dollar contract, and then stay out of training camp in his third year because the team won't renegotiate his contract. Why does he want to renegotiate? Because some other backs in the league recently signed new contracts worth more than his. He wants to renegotiate because his contract is no longer personally convenient, and he refuses to keep his commitment until he gets his way. One player recently hinted that if his contract wasn't renegotiated, he wouldn't be able to give 100 percent on the field. Can you blame him? He was only making $685,000 a year.

The spirit of our age, whether expressed in athletics, business, politics, or marriage, maintains that commitments should be honored only while convenient. When a commitment becomes inconvenient, bag it. Burton Hillis once said, "There's a mighty big difference between good, sound reasons, and reasons that sound good." Generally speaking, our society believes that only one commitment sounds good: The right to be happy.

Where were you in the turbulent sixties? Some of you were in college like I was during the latter part of that wild decade. I was raised on the San Francisco peninsula and can well remember when thousands of kids from all over the country flocked to the Haight-Ashbury district of the city by the bay. A cultural revolution took place almost overnight.

We went from short hair to long hair. We traded our corn flakes for granola and our Bass Weejuns for Earth shoes. It was important during this time to be natural and hip. Nobody wanted to be "plastic." One of the best things you could do to demonstrate your "hipness" was to get several posters and put them up in your dorm room. It was not an easy choice. One poster shop could contain hundreds of posters. And the decision was critical. It was important that the posters you chose made the right "statement."

Perhaps the most popular poster of that era portrayed a beautiful green pasture with rolling hills. The overall picture was slightly out of focus to give it an ethereal, vaporous look. There on the hill was a beautiful blonde with long, flowing hair. She wore a long, flowing dress and some beads. In the distance was a guy who (come to think of it) also had long, flowing hair and some beads. The whole scene was so hip and sixtyish. But here's the clincher. Printed on the lower left side of the poster were these words:

"You do your thing, and I'll do mine,
And if by chance we find each other,
It's beautiful."

That was so together! We thought it was great. Everybody was doing his or her own thing.

Let me offer another poem that might have appeared on the poster. This is the Farrar revised edition, and I think it's much more accurate:

"You be selfish, and I'll be selfish,
And if by chance we find each other,
It's nuclear war."

That's what should have been on the poster, because that is reality. When I do my thing, I'm selfish. When you do your thing, you're selfish. Everybody thought that poster was the ultimate in hipness, but in reality it is a formula for killing a relationship. Doing your own thing and doing what comes naturally will ultimately destroy your marriage.

The man sitting in my office never would have grown long hair, eaten granola, or traded his Florsheim Imperials for Earth shoes. He was an established Christian businessman. But he swallowed the '60s philosophy hook, line, and sinker. He was doing his own thing with this young girl, and he thought it was beautiful. He thought he had a right to be happy, and his "right" ended up destroying his family.

What about his wife of nearly forty years? Didn't she have a right to be happy, too? But he never thought about that. He was blinded by his own lust for personal gratification and thus discarded—like a worn-out pair of Nikes—the woman to whom he had once made a commitment. By claiming his "right" to be happy, he devastated the wife of his youth.

On his wedding day, he said several significant things to that woman he ultimately judged to be obsolete. He promised to be committed to her in sickness and in health, for richer or poorer, for better or worse, until death would part them. He not only made those vows to her in front of family and friends, but he gave her a ring to symbolize his lifelong commitment. Every time she would look at that ring, she would be reminded of his commitment. On his wedding day, he did everything right. Except for one thing. He didn't burn his ships.

Words that Stick

Madison Avenue is big on slogans. People are paid a lot of money to think up slogans designed to fill up the unclaimed nooks and crannies of your mind. If you can remember the slogan, they hope you will remember the product the slogan represents. Here are some current slogans making the rounds:

- The Heartbeat of America
- The Best a Man Can Get
- Tastes Great . . . Less Filling

You know the products, don't you? Chevrolet, Gillette, and Miller Lite. All you have to do is watch one ball game on TV, and those commercials are etched on your mind forever. But let me call your attention to another slogan that may not be as familiar to you: *Semper Fidelis.*

More than two hundred years ago when the

United States Marine Corps was being formed, much time was given to considering an appropriate motto. They finally chose the Latin phrase *Semper Fidelis.* Semper Fidelis is engraved on the mind of every United States marine. What does it mean? ALWAYS FAITHFUL.

Those are two powerful words. But of the two, the first is the most important, for it explains "how" a marine is to be faithful. A marine is not to be faithful only when it's personally convenient, or when the circumstances will guarantee his personal happiness. *Semper Fidelis* means *always* faithful—regardless of personal convenience or happiness.

That's why burning your ships is not a one-time event. It's not just something you do as you stand in a rented tuxedo before a group of your friends and family. Burning your ships is something you do every day of your life.

Did you run track in high school? Perhaps you ran the 95-yard dash, or the 215. I didn't run track myself, but I had several friends who did. And as I recall, none of them ran the 95 or the 215. Several of them, however, competed in the 100-yard dash and the 220.

The point is this: In marriage, as well as the Christian life, it's not how you start that counts, it's how you finish. You can run your heart out for 95 yards and even lead the field, but if you stop five yards short, those 95 yards were an exercise in futility. Too many men in our society are running the 95-yard dash in their marriages. And if you run only 35, 50, 65, or even 95, and then quit, you have wasted your time. Commitment means you suck it up and finish.

If we are going to save our boys, then we must make a personal commitment to finish the race. It's a commitment we renew every morning. If they don't see us finish the race, why should they?

It is much better for a boy to learn the meaning of *Semper Fidelis* from the example of his father than from a drill sergeant in boot camp. A boy who has a father who is committed to his mother will have a tremendous advantage when he becomes a husband. He will have an intuitive understanding that his commitment in marriage is not a right to be happy, but to demonstrate a willingness to be responsible. Even when it's inconvenient. Even when it crowds out his personal happiness.

If you are to have any hope of saving your boys for the next generation, you will

- from this day forward adopt as your personal motto, *Semper Fidelis*;
- from this day forward burn your ships.

A One-Woman Kind of Man

Burning your ships sounds great. But how do you do it?

The way to burn your ships in the war on the family is to become a one-woman kind of man. First Timothy 3:1-7 and Titus 1:5-9 describe the character qualifications necessary for spiritual leaders in the church (elders and pastors). The same qualification is required for deacons (1 Timothy 3:12).

An elder is a spiritually mature man who gives oversight to the church with other qualified men. Both passages insist that an elder must be the husband of one wife. That has led to much debate over whether a divorced man could serve in this position. It is not my purpose here to discuss that issue.

I want you to note that phrase, "the husband of one wife." That phrase could be literally translated, "a one-woman kind of man." That is really the sense of the statement. One of the primary qualifications for a leader in the church is that he must be a one-woman kind of man. A one-woman kind of man is a man who has adopted the motto *Semper Fidelis.* A one-woman kind of man is a man who reminds himself every day that he has burned his ships.

Some of you reading this had a father who was not committed to your mother. Maybe your dad made it a practice to be involved from time to time with other women. Or maybe your father was committed to your mom, but just wasn't around enough to model it for you. In other words, you may be confused about what a one-woman kind of man is, simply because you've never seen one in action.

What does it mean to be a one-woman kind of man? The answer is critical, because if we are going to save the boys we must first save our marriages. And the secret to saving your marriage—even if you never serve in a church as elder or deacon—is to become a one-woman kind of man.

A One-Woman Kind of Man Is Committed with His Eyes

Do you remember the song "I Only Have Eyes For You"? Over the years it has been recorded by everyone from the Flamingos to Art Garfunkel.

My love must be a special kind of blind love,
I can't see anyone but you,

Are the stars out tonight?
I don't know if it's cloudy or bright,
    I only have eyes for you, dear . . .

The moon may be high,
but I can't see a thing in the sky,
    I only have eyes for you . . .

I don't know if we're in a garden,
    or on a crowded avenue,
    You are here, so am I,
        maybe millions of people go by,
But they all disappear from view,
    And I only have eyes for you . . .[1]

That should be the theme song of every Christian man in America. The very first line of the song captures the essence of what it means to be a one-woman kind of man: My love *must* be a special kind of blind love. . . .

It doesn't mean that a guy doesn't see or notice other women. That's impossible. But because of our commitment to be a one-woman kind of man with our eyes, we don't look at other women in a way that would diminish our commitment to our wife. A one-woman kind of man has purposefully cultivated a special kind of blindness.

In the Old Testament, Job put it this way: "I made a covenant with my eyes not to look lustfully at a girl" (Job 31:1). Job is making a commitment to a special kind of blind love. He's burning his ships. He's talking *Semper Fidelis*.

Let's carefully observe what Job is saying here. He isn't making a commitment to never *notice* an attractive female. That would not only be ludicrous, but would require total blindness. Good-looking girls and women are everywhere. You can't help but see them.

There is a difference, however, between seeing a beautiful woman and lusting after her. Job's point is simply this: There is a difference between a look and a *lustful* look.

C.S. Lewis once said, "If you look upon ham and eggs and lust, you have already committed breakfast in your heart." Whether it's an attractive woman or a heaping plate of cholesterol, the principle is the same. There is a difference between looking and looking with lust.

A one-woman kind of man is a man who demonstrates his commitment by disciplining his eyes. We are all familiar with the guy who can't walk one block without giving some woman the once-over from head to toe. He will even stop dead in his tracks in the flow of pedestrian traffic to turn and watch her as she goes by. Most of us are a little better socially adjusted than that.

A man who is committed with his eyes will avoid certain kinds of magazines and television programs. I'm writing this in a hotel room in Chicago, hundreds of miles from my wife and kids. A hotel room on the road can be a very dangerous place for a one-woman kind of man who is not prepared for battle.

When I bought a newspaper at the hotel gift shop this morning, it was surrounded by pornographic magazines with alluring covers. "Girls of the Southwest Conference!" blazed the cover. If I don't discipline my eyes and look away, I'm going to start wondering how those girls in the Southwest Conference are getting along. But I'm committed to a special kind of blind love. I must particularly cultivate that blindness away from home. I know I must do this because I know myself. And the self I know has a hard enough time even when I'm *not* away from home.

Years ago as a rookie pastor in my first church, I met with a group of guys every Tuesday night. After the meeting, I went with one of them to a local coffee shop. It was the coldest night of the year, and I was freezing so I did something I never do. I ordered a cup of hot coffee. I never drink coffee. In a year's time I may drink three or four cups max. No kidding. I just don't like the stuff. But on that particular night, as we sat there and talked I was so cold that I had at least five cups of cream and sugar with my coffee.

I got home about 10:30, watched the late sports on the news, and went to bed. I couldn't go to sleep; I was wide awake. After about an hour, I went downstairs and turned on Carson. When Carson was over, I went back to bed, but no luck. I was so wired on caffeine, I couldn't blink my eyes, let alone close them. So I got up and read the new *Sports Illustrated* that came in the mail that afternoon. Now it was around 2 A.M., and I went upstairs to give it another try. At three o'clock, I got up to see if there was an old movie on the tube. There wasn't.

I was getting a little ticked by this time. I had read everything in the house, and there was nothing on TV. Then I got an idea. My subscription to *Time* had recently run out, and I decided to visit the local twenty-four hour convenience store to see if they had the new one. So off I went at 3:30 A.M. to find a *Time* magazine.

As I was looking for *Time*, I picked up *Newsweek* and flipped through it, then *US News and World*

Report, and before I realized it I had picked up *Playboy* and was rapidly turning its pages. Suddenly, I came to my senses and thought, *What in the world am I doing? What if my wife were to see me doing this, or someone in my congregation? What kind of pastor would do something like this? I'm standing here like some kind of adolescent trying to get some jollies.* I felt utterly ashamed as I put down that magazine. I looked around and saw no one else in the store but the clerk. I assure you that I had not planned to pick up that magazine when I went into that store. But I did it. I'd been picked off in a weak moment.

As I was preaching the next Sunday, one of my points dealt with integrity. I commented on how easy it is to teach the truth without applying it to your own life. My greatest fear is to fall into the trap of teaching the very thing I am disobeying. So I did something extreme. I told the congregation what had happened to me on Tuesday night. I told them the whole story. I asked them to forgive me for being such a poor example. And that extreme decision helped me to decide that I never wanted to have that kind of humiliating experience again.

I learned a valuable lesson from that situation. From that point on, I developed a plan as to how I would handle pornographic material before ever entering any store or newsstand. I had to have a plan in place to defeat the sexual temptation that comes to me through my eyes. I learned that I must anticipate and determine how I will act before I ever get into a tempting situation.

It was embarrassing to have to stand before my congregation and tell them what I had done. But I decided it was better to be embarrassed than to stand

and preach a lie. I wanted to be honest with them and let them know that none of us are exempt from temptation at a weak moment. I wanted to be one-woman kind of man. But in that situation, I wasn't. I let my wife down.

A one-woman kind of man *must* have a predetermined plan fixed in his mind so he can withstand the sneak attacks of the enemy. We never know when we are going to be tempted with our eyes. That's why the plan must be *predetermined*. We must anticipate a tempting situation in advance and decide beforehand how we will deal with it. That's the principle behind civil defense. It's also the principle of sexual defense.

Let's talk about traveling one more time. I've found that many guys really have a tough time when they're away from home.

As I write at this desk in a hotel room in Chicago, just four feet from my chair is a television with a card on top advertising five pay movies. Two of them are pornographic. I could reach over right now, flip on the TV, and punch in the wrong channel and have instant pornography. *And no one would ever know.* My wife would never know, my kids would never know, my friends would never know. But when I recited my vows to Mary years ago, I burned my ships. I had to burn them again this morning.

Sometimes it takes extreme measures to be a one-woman kind of man with your eyes. I recently read about a man who took unusual steps to maintain his special kind of blind love. This Christian businessman does a fair amount of traveling and has come to the conclusion that his ability to fight temptation on the road tends to weaken after about three days.

If he's going to be in a hotel longer than three days, he calls the hotel to make a request. He asks the manager to remove the TV from his room. Usually the manager says they can't do that. The man then politely points out that the maintenance man could do it in a matter of minutes. If the manager wants this man's business for five or six nights of lodging, the set will have to go.

The problem for most men is not *working* on the road. It is the *leisure time* we have on the road. W.T. Taylor exuded wisdom when he said, "Temptation rarely comes in working hours. It is in their leisure time that men are made or marred."

Removing a television set is extreme. But I respect such a man. He knows himself and recognizes his weakness. He knows that after a long day of exhausting meetings or sales calls, he is especially susceptible with his leisure time. So in order to keep himself in check, he takes extreme measures. Why? *Semper Fidelis.*

Jesus Himself advocated taking extreme measures in certain situations:

> You have heard that it was said, "You shall not commit adultery"; but I say to you, that everyone who looks on a woman to lust for her has committed adultery with her already in his heart.

> And if your right eye makes you stumble, tear it out, and throw it from you; for it is better for you that one of the parts of your body perish, than for your whole body to be thrown into hell.

> And if your right hand makes you stumble,

cut it off, and throw it from you; for it is better for you that one of the parts of your
body perish, than for your whole body to go
into hell (Matthew 5:27-30, NASB).

Notice that Jesus didn't say that if your eye
offends you, put on sunglasses. He didn't suggest that
if your right hand causes you to stumble, put it in an
Ace bandage. He used hyperbole to make a clear
statement. Hyperbole is the use of extravagant exag-
geration to make a point. Notice that Jesus is making
the same point we noticed earlier. He is talking about
looking at a woman with lust.

The obvious lesson is that we must deal with the
source of the temptation. You can pluck your eye out
if you want. But it might be just as effective to unbolt
the TV next time you're at the Marriott. The principle
our Lord is teaching is simply this: There are times in
the Christian life when extreme action is not only
appropriate, but necessary.

I've had to learn to be prepared for temptation
when I travel without my wife. I'm talking Red Alert,
Code 1. When I check into a hotel, I am prepared for
battle. I am like a marine ready to hit the beach at Iwo
Jima. I'm wearing camouflage combat fatigues, my face
is greased, I've got an M-16 and a full set of pearl-
handled socket wrenches with my initials engraved on
the handle (you never know what size bolts you're
going to come across).

I draw up my battle plan before I ever walk out
my front door. My strategy is clear, and the tactics are
non-negotiable. Before I ever walk into the hotel, I
have predetermined how I will respond to the pornography that surrounds the newspapers on the news-

stand. I have determined in advance that I would no more pick up a pornographic magazine than I would a live grenade.

I have decided in advance how I am going to handle the temptation of private pornographic television. Your tactics may be to unbolt the set or to throw a bedspread over it. Or maybe you can write down in your Daytimer a log of every TV show you watch while on your business trip. When you get home, show it to your wife or to your pastor. That will force you to explain your actions. It will also keep you from sin.

Extreme, you say? You bet. And that's exactly what Jesus was telling us to do.

I can promise you this: If we don't get extreme with the temptation of our eyes, then it will get extreme with us.

A One-Woman Kind of Man Is Committed with His Mind

The major battlefield in spiritual warfare is the mind. The mind is the line of scrimmage in the Christian life, and whoever controls the line of scrimmage controls the game. The mind is where the enemy seeks to control us. If he can influence our minds, he can influence our behavior.

It was Oscar Wilde who said, "I can resist anything except temptation." It was Franklin Jones who wrote, "What makes resisting temptation difficult for many people is they don't want to discourage it completely."

The apostle Paul had a different kind of outlook when he wrote: "For though we live in the world, we do not wage war as the world does. The weapons we fight with are not the weapons of the world. On the contrary, they have divine power to demolish strongholds. We demolish arguments and every pretension that sets itself up against the knowledge of God, and we take captive every thought to make it obedient to Christ" (2 Corinthians 10:3-5).

All kinds of sophisticated philosophies are out there. A man who wants to lead his family must learn to sift through the wrong ideas and take them captive to the obedience of Christ. Bill Hull writes that a man "must know the Bible well enough, through study, to fight temptation and protect himself against the ideas and philosophies of the world. [He] is confronted daily with thousands of messages and ideas. A biblical defense system must sort out the ideas, take what is obedient to Christ, and reject what is not."[2]

Every war has its captives, and in this war the objective is to capture wrong thoughts and patterns of thinking. An evil philosophy lurks behind the enemy's attempt to lure us into sexual lust, and we must be wise enough to capture those wrong thoughts for Christ. Temptation itself is not sin, but a call to battle. In this battle as in any other, the objective is to take as many captives as possible. Let's specifically apply Paul's admonition to the man who wants to be committed to his wife in his thought life.

Such a man protects himself from thinking or fantasizing about other women. This is a constant and perpetual battle. Christian men will deal with this nearly every day of their lives.

Let's put this battle into perspective. First—and this is very important—*you cannot prevent wrong thoughts from coming into your mind.* That's temptation. It is not wrong to be tempted. Jesus was tempted but was without sin. You have not sinned when you are tempted. You should not feel guilty when you are tempted. If you do, that is false guilt. Genuine guilt is the result of sin.

Imagine you're back at the hotel newsstand. On your way to the coffee shop for breakfast, you go by the gift shop to pick up *USA Today*. As your eyes sweep the newsstand looking for that specific paper, you see an alluring cover advertising the girls of the Southwest Conference. As you see it, the thought immediately crosses your mind that this magazine may be something worth seeing. That's temptation.

Now let's stop the video tape right here and ask a question. Has sin taken place at this point? No. What has taken place is temptation. The thought to violate your commitment to Christ and your wife by picking up the magazine has flashed in your mind. It is not a sin to have that thought. At this moment, sin has not occurred. But what you do with that thought in the next microsecond will determine whether that thought will turn into sin.

So far, you've only seen the ham and eggs. You haven't yet decided to lust.

As your eyes come into contact with the magazine and the tempter suggests you pick it up, you must make a choice. Do you give in to the wrong thought, allow your eyes and mind to do what is wrong, or do you take that thought captive to the obedience of Christ? It is that instantaneous reaction to temptation that determines whether we turn the thought into sin or into obedience.

There is no sin in seeing the ham and eggs. But if you decide to linger over the ham and eggs, you have just committed breakfast in your heart.

These wrong thoughts are the grenades of the enemy. He hurls them into our minds at the most unexpected and surprising moments. You cannot stop them from coming. But you can develop a habit of capturing them and turning them into opportunities to obey Christ.

Don't get discouraged if you are having a tough time with your thought life. It normally takes time to begin making progress.

Learning to deal with wrong thoughts is like learning to dribble with your left hand. One of the regrets of my life is that I never mastered the art of dribbling with my left hand. As a result, most of the time I drive to my right. After several minutes, the guy defending me gets the picture. Every once in a while, I try to go to my left, but I don't have the control or the confidence I need to be effective.

I like to shoot around in the backyard with my kids. Although our small, makeshift court on our patio is anything but regulation, we have a lot of fun shooting baskets out there. Last year, I decided I was going to help my eight-year-old, John, develop his left hand. John is right-handed, so as we would play he would naturally dribble with his right hand. He rarely attempted to dribble with his left. I encouraged him to try it several times, and he hated it. It was just too hard. It wasn't natural for him.

Then I decided to change my approach. John and I like to play one-on-one, so I decided to make a rule change. For every dribble with his left hand before making a basket, I would multiply the two points for the basket by the number of times he dribbled with his left hand. If he dribbled with his left hand three times, then the basket was worth six points instead of two. If he dribbled with his left five times, a bucket was good for ten points.

I purposely guarded him by standing to his right, forcing him to take the opening to his left. At first, he got discouraged as the ball bounced off his foot and veered into the bushes. I remember his intense frustration in trying to learn this new and foreign skill. On more than one occasion, he blurted out, "I'll never get it!" But I kept encouraging him, and gave him some openings to his right to make him feel better.

Nevertheless, I continued to position myself so he had to drive to his left. As the weeks went by, he started getting four-point baskets, and then six pointers. After several months, he actually dribbled nine times with his left hand and scored. I was down 18 to 0, and he had taken one shot.

Last summer, John went to a morning basketball camp put on by the local college coach and his staff. When I got home one day, John was ecstatic. He told me about a drill they all did that morning. The coach put out six pylons spaced out over a half-court area. Each boy had to dribble around the pylons to half court with his right hand, then switch to his left coming back. John won the competition going away. He said "Dad, just about everybody could do it with their right hand, but they all slowed down coming back with their left."

Why did John win that competition? I'll tell you why. John won the drill because he had developed a new habit.

The point is this: Learning to deal with your thought life is the spiritual equivalent of learning to dribble with your left hand. You will not be successful at first. You will feel overwhelmed, discouraged, and frustrated. You will begin to think you will never make progress. But slowly and surely, you will develop a new habit. It doesn't come easy, but what worthwhile habit does? You will be developing a new pattern of thinking.

> Sow a thought, reap an act;
> Sow an act, reap a habit;
> Sow a habit, reap a character;
> Sow a character, reap a destiny.

If you have spent twenty-five years giving in to sexual lust, don't expect to turn things around in three weeks. But if you keep going to your left in your thought-life, eventually you won't have to think about it as much. You'll never be perfect, but you can develop some very strong automatic responses to sexual temptation.

Perhaps until now the temptations have consistently captured you. But as you devote yourself to this discipline you will begin to capture your thoughts. And as you work to capture your thoughts, you'll develop spiritual muscle and character.

As far as I can tell, there's only one way to do that. And here it is:

Aggressively attack.

You have to get aggressive in your approach to temptation. Too many of us have lowered our standards and given ourselves unspoken permission to fail with sexual temptation. We have to make a decision that will get as aggressive against sin as Dick Butkus got against fullbacks.

Have you ever seen that NFL highlight film on the career of Dick Butkus? Butkus became a living legend because of his aggressiveness. He was unbelievable. He would spit, kick, punch, jab, knee, trip, clothesline, or bite anyone who got in his way.

Why was he so aggressive? Because his objective was to attack the ball-carrier. Butkus didn't just want to tackle the runner, he wanted to remove the guy's helmet with his head still inside. He wanted to cave-in the halfback's chest. He wanted to make sure that quarterback would never throw another pass in his life.

When you face sexual temptation, you have to turn into a Butkus. This is no time to eat quiche and sip Perrier. There you are, number 51, standing over the center, with steam snorting out of your nostrils. You know that a 240-pound running back of temptation is coming right up the middle with the intention of imprinting his cleats on your chest. As soon as that wrong thought is snapped, you have to step into that hole, take on the 285-pound guard with steroids swimming in his bloodstream, and stuff him while simultaneously clotheslining the back as he tries to get by on your left. You have to capture that wrong thought the same way Butkus would obliterate running backs.

Gentlemen, we must get aggressive toward temptation. We must snort, grunt, and snarl if necessary, but we absolutely cannot be passive. We must adopt an attack mentality.

The next time you are tempted to think illicit sexual thoughts, you must attack. You must get aggressive and hit. When that wrong thought enters your mind, you hit it like Butkus. You capture, seize, gouge, and strangle it to the obedience of Christ.

There are two things you must do. First, look away from the temptation. You made a covenant with your eyes, remember? *Semper Fidelis.*

Second, let me suggest something completely wild. Immediately begin to pray for that woman. Seize the wrong thought and begin to pray that if she doesn't know Christ, she will come to know his love and forgiveness. If she's married, pray for the relationship she has with her husband, that their marriage would be protected from the attacks of the evil one. If she's single, pray that God would keep her pure and clean for the man she might someday marry.

I think you get the point. You cannot pray and lust at the same time. By aggressively seizing the wrong thought, you can turn it into an opportunity to bless that woman, not use her. After all, you're a one-woman kind of man. And you have burned your ships.

A one-woman kind of man is committed with his eyes and with his thought life. But there are three other characteristics that complete our description of a one-woman man. These next three descriptions will be brief; just three vignettes (by the way, that's how I like my salads . . . just a little oil and vignette).

A One-Woman Man Is Faithful with His Lips

A man committed to his wife is no flirt. He doesn't play junior high games with other women. He doesn't kid around about being interested in someone else. He doesn't make jokes about getting together with other women.

Such jesting can all come under the umbrella of having a few harmless laughs. But some things are off-limits. Marriage is one of them. Marriage is sacred. Marriage is holy. It's nothing to kid around about.

A One-Woman Man Is Faithful with His Hands

When I was a kid, my mom used to tell me to "keep my hands to myself." Usually I had just criminally assaulted one of my brothers.

Keeping your hands to yourself is a great piece of advice if you want to be a one-woman kind of man. A one-woman man is careful how he touches the opposite sex. Why is he careful? Because he's committed to one woman. *Semper Fidelis.*

As a rule of thumb, I usually don't hug other women. That presents a problem because a lot of Christians like to hug. Whenever I say this, I usually push somebody's button, and the other person gets upset and thinks I'm not loving or kind. But that's not it.

Mary and I have some close friends we love dearly. When we run into each other, it's not uncommon for me to hug my friend's wife as a greeting, and for him to hug Mary. But generally speaking, I don't hug women. Why not? Because I want to be a one-woman kind of man, and the way I figure it, that means hugging one woman.

The real reason I'm bringing this up is that I've noticed a correlation between verbal flirting and flirting that includes touching . . . even "harmless" touching. I knew one church deacon who, with his wife, greeted everyone at the door on Sunday mornings. I watched his wife's embarrassed expression as he would hug and stroke (in a spiritual way) every attractive woman who came in. He was always joking around about meeting some woman at a hotel or getting together for dinner. Just kidding, of course.

I guess that's why I wasn't surprised when he ran off with the youth director's wife. He never was a one-woman kind of man, and it showed.

You know as well as I do that a hug can come from the purest of motives. But it can come also from wrong motives. There's nothing wrong with a hug. But next time you think about hugging a woman, and you're not sure about your motives, don't. If you want to hug somebody, go find your wife.

A One-Woman Man Is Committed with His Feet

First Corinthians 6:18 says it flat out: "Flee from sexual immorality." That's how a one-woman man deals with movies, magazines, videos, or any kind of situation that is counterproductive to marriage commitment. He flees.

Someone has said that most men who flee temptation usually leave a forwarding address. That won't cut it if you're going to be a one-woman kind of man. A one-woman man doesn't hang around to check out a pornographic magazine for its artistic value. He doesn't hesitate to walk out of a movie that violates his value system. He takes the lead in turning off the TV or the VCR when it's appropriate. That's what it means to flee. A one-woman man uses his feet to demonstrate his commitment.

Fleeing from immorality means we are willing to do different things in different situations. It could mean that you will

get on the bus, Gus
make a new plan, Stan
drop off the key, Lee
and get yourself free.

That's what Gus, Stan, and Lee may have to do if they are going to flee immorality.

That describes a one-woman kind of man. A one-woman man is committed with his mind, his eyes, his lips, his hands, and his feet. If we are going to protect ourselves from the epidemic of adultery, we must understand the process that leads to adultery. David sinned with his eyes, his mind, his lips, and his hands before he ever did with his sexual organ. That's where David lost the battle. Not when he finally hit the sheets with Bathsheba.

Adultery does not begin with the sexual organ, it begins with the mind. And the man who renews his commitment to his wife each day is a man of holiness and a lethal weapon in the hands of God.

Well, that's it. That's what a one-woman man looks like. He burns his ships. He practices *Semper Fidelis*. He hits wrong thoughts like Butkus after a wide-receiver. He only has eyes for her, his lips are sealed, his hands are tied, and his feet are quick. That's the kind of energy it takes to stay away from adultery.

CHAPTER FIVE

Anorexic Men and Their Bulimic Cousins

We owe to Scripture the same reverence which we owe to God.

John Calvin

Introductions are supposed to be short. Any communicator will tell you that. I'm going to violate that principle in this chapter. This may be the longest introduction in the history of Western civilization.

I need to shoot straight with you. There's a good chance I'm going to lose you either in this chapter or the next. I was up until 2 A.M. last night trying to figure out how I could keep that from happening. Mary asked if anything was bothering me, and I told her my problem. I told her I was trying to come up with a solution to keep people reading. Then she said, "Why don't you just tell them about it up front?" Not a bad idea.

The reason the next two chapters are so critical is that without the biblical principles they contain, you can *never* be a spiritual leader in your home. Never. This entire book is based on the assumption that it is impossible to effectively lead your home unless you become a spiritual self-starter. These next two chapters will explain the two indispensable requirements for becoming a spiritual self-starter.

You may agree with everything that has been said up to now, but if you do not grasp the next two subjects and implement them, you won't be an effective leader. That's why I couldn't sleep last night. To say that these two chapters are important is a huge understatement.

I'm not trying to con you into staying with this book. This isn't some carefully crafted psychological ploy to keep your interest. I'm not that smart. I'm just telling you the truth. The enemy does not want you to interact with these two principles. I know he does not want me to write them. If you had any idea how much resistance I encountered in trying to write these chapters, you could probably guess how much resistance you'll meet in attempting to read and apply them.

This is where the rubber meets the road. This is what separates the men from the boys. Some of you will read this and say to yourselves, "I've heard this before," and stop reading. You probably have heard it before, but the question is, do you practice it? Research in my file proves that most Christian men don't.

It is exactly at these two points that the enemy neutralizes most Christian men. In the first chapter I mentioned the enemy has two primary strategies in the war on the family. The first is to effectively alienate and sever the relationship between husband and wife. The second is to effectively alienate and sever the relationship between father and children. But there is a third strategy he uses with deadly effectiveness.

Strategy #3: *To effectively sever and alienate a man from the spiritual disciplines that will keep him fit and effective for spiritual battle.*

It is right here that Satan keeps a man from reaching his full potential for Christ. You may be active in the church, you may be doctrinally pure, you may even be serving on the church board, but if you are not involved in these two disciplines, your impact will be minimal. Minimal on your family and minimal in your church. The enemy does not mind if you are spiritually active. He just doesn't want you to be spiritually *effective*. Spiritual activity does not equal spiritual effectiveness.

Without question, these next two chapters are the toughest in the book. If you can get through these, the remaining chapters will be a piece of cake. Don't get me wrong—these two chapters aren't that tough to understand. The problem is they're difficult to apply, and application's the name of the game in the Christian life. Without it, we're just playing games . . . and you and I both know that leading a family in this culture is no game.

Okay. That's it. End of introduction. In fact, we might as well start this chapter over.

Anorexic Men and Their Bulimic Cousins

*We owe to Scripture the same reverence
which we owe to God.*

John Calvin

A lot of rock stars die young. It seems to go with the territory. Whether it's from a plane crash or a drug overdose, it seems to happen frequently.

Still, it was especially stunning to read the newspaper on February 4, 1983, to find that Karen Carpenter had died at the age of thirty-two. What was even more baffling was what killed her. It wasn't a plane crash, and it wasn't a drug overdose. Karen Carpenter died from *anorexia nervosa*.

When we heard the news, most of us said,

"What?" It was the first time many of us had ever heard of the sickness. Karen Carpenter had been anorexic for years, and most of us had no idea what the illness was.

Anorexia nervosa is extreme body emaciation caused by an emotional or psychological aversion to food and eating. The condition occurs predominantly in young women whose body weight may drop to half of normal. In contrast to victims of famine, sufferers from anorexia nervosa are often able to maintain their strength and daily activities at approximately normal levels. They appear to be unconcerned with their undernourished state and do not feel hungry. In laymen's terms, a young woman with anorexia nervosa avoids food.

I'm convinced there is such a thing as spiritual anorexia—and the enemy has been incredibly successful in spreading it. In the spiritual realm, it is not partial to women. Thousands of Christian men have spiritual anorexia, and that is why they are ineffective in leading their families. What is spiritual anorexia? *Spiritual anorexia is an aversion to reading the Scriptures.*

We have all seen tragic pictures of starving children in Ethiopia. Many of them are so weak they cannot stand up. Anorexic men are just as weak spiritually as those children are physically. Why? They both lack nutritious food.

The words of Jesus recorded in Matthew 4:4 prove the point: "Man does not live on bread alone, but on *every word* that comes from the mouth of God."

Observe carefully the words of Deuteronomy 32:46-47: "Take to heart all the words I have solemnly declared to you this day, so that you may command your children to obey carefully all the words of this law. They are not just idle words for you—they *are your life.*" No wonder the enemy wants to keep us from the Scriptures.

C.S. Lewis wrote a wonderful little book titled *The Screwtape Letters.* The book records the letters of an old and wise demon named Screwtape to his young nephew Wormwood, a rookie at spiritual warfare. Wormwood has been assigned to influence a certain man away from Christianity. Lewis cleverly and humorously describes the different methods the enemy will employ to keep us from any kind of spiritual growth. It's a wonderful book that contains much insight and wisdom.

But as Dr. Martyn Lloyd-Jones has pointed out, it has one major defect. Lewis does not deal with the question of reading the Word of God. The crafty old uncle gives no instruction to his young nephew about keeping his intended victim away from the Bible. Yet this is precisely what the enemy attempts to do. It may be his primary goal. He will go to any extreme to keep us from taking in Scripture. This is one of his most consistent tactics, and he is relentless in it. He does not want us reading God's Word. He wants us spiritually anorexic.

George Gallup, the famous pollster, is a committed Christian who was recently interviewed by *Leadership* magazine. *Leadership* asked Gallup whether any of his poll results had surprised him. "Oh yes," he answered. "I'm amazed at the low level of Bible knowledge. It's shocking to see that only 42 percent know that Jesus was the one who delivered the Sermon on the Mount . . . Are they reading the Bible?

From our studies, the Bible is clearly not being read. It's revered, but not read."[1]

Gallup is describing spiritual anorexia. The vast majority of men I know who are spiritual anorexics believe that the Bible is inspired by God. Most of them own several translations of the Bible, including at least one study Bible. They hold it in high esteem, yet they rarely read it. Except at church. When they remember to bring it.

When I was working on my doctorate, I asked more than a thousand Christian men across the United States how often in an average week they interacted with the Lord through the Scriptures. Forty-five percent reported one time a week or less. The majority of these men are committed Christians and attend church more than once a week. They are not on the fringes of the church. Most would be considered pillars of their local congregations. Yet nearly half of them are spiritually anorexic.

Is it possible that nearly fifty percent of the Christian men who are called to lead their families are spiritually anorexic? Probably to a man they would tell you they revere God's Word. My friend, the enemy does not mind if you revere the Bible, just so long as you don't feed from it. He will do whatever he can to keep you from interacting with the Scripture.

For a number of years, I was a spiritual anorexic. I wasn't growing in my Christian life, and no wonder. My intake of the Word was hit and miss. I always meant to read the Scripture, but somehow other things crowded out my time. I would plan on reading Scripture just before I went to bed, but by the time I hit the sack I was just too tired. *I'll get up early and do it in the morning*, I would say to myself. But when morning came, it got crowded out again. Day after day, week after week, month after month, I had the best of intentions. But somehow I never got into a consistent pattern. It took several years before I realized I was cutting myself off from the only source of spiritual nutrition. I had to change my priorities.

As a result, I made a personal commitment to begin each day by reading Scripture. I've been doing this now for years. And yet every single morning, I am tempted to skip my reading. Amazing! Allow me to describe the situation.

As I come down the stairs, straight ahead of me is the front door. I know that just outside that door is a fresh, brand new, hot-off-the-press newspaper. I love newspapers. I love to scan the front page, then turn to the sports section and drink in every word. My idea of a great vacation is to go where I can get a copy of the *Los Angeles Times* (my favorite newspaper), then spend the first hour of each day reading through its immensity.

Every morning at home, as I step off the stairs, I have to make a decision. What I *want* to do is open the door and pick up the paper. What I *need* to do is make a left turn, go over to the bookshelf in the family room, and get my Bible. Every single morning, it's the same dilemma! Nearly every morning of my life, I have to make a conscious effort to read the Bible. You'd think it would get easier the longer I make that choice. But it doesn't, at least not for me. The temptation to do something else is always there.

I consider my time in the Word to be a morning briefing. Before I go out to face the day, I need to be briefed by the Lord. The briefing serves different functions.

First, *it reminds me that there is a God who is ruling the affairs of my life.*

Society lives as though there is no God, and I need to be reminded before I face the day that there is a God who is in control of my life and circumstances.

Second, *I need to be reminded of what is true.*

God's Word gives me a dose of reality. There is right and wrong; there are consequences for making wrong choices; the Ten Commandments are still the standard for life; I am not to repay evil for evil; etc. My morning briefing gives a perspective that I don't get in the world. I need God's commentary on life every day. A Christian man in this society is swimming upstream against the current. Without the constant nutrition of the Word, he will soon tire and be dragged off by the sheer force of the current.

A solid education of biblical truth is no option for the family leader. Samuel Johnson put it this way: "The supreme end of education is expert discernment in all things—the power to tell the good from the bad, the genuine from the counterfeit, and to prefer the good and the genuine to the bad and the counterfeit." The Bible gives me that discernment every morning that I open its pages.

Third, *the morning briefing reinforces my convictions.*

It's not easy to hold onto convictions when you're in the minority. You and I live in a society that is constantly trying to chip away at our biblical convictions. My time in the Scripture each morning underscores why I hold those convictions. We are in a war for our families, and we cannot afford to compromise the divine absolutes given us. When a soldier begins to question his convictions about the morality of his cause, his effectiveness vanishes. That's precisely what happened to some of our soldiers in Vietnam.

As I read and ponder the Scriptures, I am forced to evaluate my convictions. Perhaps some of them don't agree with God's Word and need to be changed. Or maybe I've started to compromise convictions I've always held. As I am exposed to Scripture, I find encouragement to stand firm in the truth and not negotiate what the Bible clearly teaches. Each day I have to make choices based on my convictions. That is why it is vital not to miss the morning briefing. I need God's input to make consistently right choices.

I must feed on Scripture every day, just as a soldier on the front lines must eat K rations. I must have a steady diet of spiritual vitamins and minerals if I am going to be in any condition to fight. I cannot afford to be spiritually anorexic when I've been given the responsibility to lead my family. A malnourished man is worthless in hand-to-hand combat. Because he has no strength, he is easy prey for the enemy.

Bulimic Men

As dangerous as anorexia is, something else afflicting Christian men is even worse. It is spiritual bulimia.

To understand spiritual bulimia, we must take a look at the physical variety. Dr. Raymond Vath describes it this way: "Bulimia is an illness with recurrent, compulsive episodes of binge eating followed by self-induced vomiting and/or purging with laxatives."[2]

This disorder, too, normally afflicts young women. But spiritual bulimia is especially contagious to Christian men.

118

Spiritually speaking, bulimia is the inconsistent reading or hearing of the Word without personal application. A young girl with bulimia will binge and take in a tremendous amount of food, only to quickly vomit, thus denying her body the nutrients it needs.

The danger in the Christian life comes when I listen to a sermon or go to a Christian seminar or listen to a series of teaching tapes without applying the truth I hear to my life. That is spiritual bulimia.

Spiritual bulimia is an aversion to applying the Scripture to my life. Scriptural facts may be in my mind, but I am not integrating them into my life. I am chewing the food and swallowing it, but only for awhile. Then I get rid of the food, preventing digestion. Without digestion, I cannot benefit from the nutrients in the food. Without meditation leading to application, there is no spiritual digestion, and I continue to lose strength.

Let me explain it from a different angle. The opposite of up is down. The opposite of happy is sad. The opposite of on is off. Now let me ask you something. What is the opposite of ignorance? "Knowledge," you say.

When people come to know Jesus Christ as Lord and Savior, they are spiritual infants. They are spiritually ignorant. That's why we put them into Sunday school classes, small group Bible studies, hand them several good tapes, and tell them when they can hear some good Bible teaching on the radio. Those are all very good ideas. We do this so they can move from spiritual ignorance to spiritual knowledge.

But here is where we sometimes make a critical mistake . . . and plant the seeds of spiritual bulimia. As

Howard Hendricks has pointed out, in the Christian life the opposite of ignorance is not knowledge, but *obedience*. God does not want to take a new Christian and move him from ignorance to knowledge. He wants to move him from ignorance to knowledge *to obedience*. Do you remember James 1:22? James says, "But prove yourselves doers of the word, and not merely hearers who delude themselves" (NASB).

James describes spiritual bulimia. The man who hears the Word of God has received knowledge. But knowledge is not the goal, the goal is to *do* the Word. The man must obey. It is foolish to hear the Word without obeying it. In the Christian life, it is God's plan to move us from ignorance to knowledge to obedience. Obedience means that I apply His Word to my life and circumstances. If I don't do that, then I am binging and purging. I am eating the Word and running into some bathroom to throw up the spiritual truth I've just heard.

Do you remember the two men I described earlier in this book? The first left a well-paying professional position to take a much smaller salary working for a Christian organization. He was the one studying the Christian book on marriage with his secretary. Chapter after chapter in that book identified principles from Scripture designed to help a man grow in his love for his wife. This guy read those chapters and got so excited that he would tell other people to buy the book. Then he would go where no one was watching and vomit up the scriptural truths that so excited him.

The second man I described was in his early sixties, a respected Christian leader in the community who left his wife of forty years for a girl younger than his daughters. That man was a spiritual bulimic. He would sit in church every Sunday and listen carefully to make sure the sermon was doctrinally pure. Then he would go home, vomit the Word of God, and call his girlfriend. He knew the Word. He just didn't do it. That is spiritual bulimia.

Both men sought scriptural knowledge. Both appeared to have an appetite for spiritual truth. Both had "quiet times." And both left their families. Why? Because both thought the goal was to go from spiritual ignorance to spiritual knowledge. It isn't. The goal is to go from ignorance to knowledge to obedience. While they were both "hearers" of the Word, neither were doers.

You don't have to commit adultery to be spiritually bulimic. A person has spiritual bulimia when he consistently refuses to apply a known scriptural principle to his life.

Ezra was neither anorexic or bulimic. The Scripture simply states that, "Ezra had set his heart to study the law of the LORD, and to practice it" (Ezra 7:10, NASB). That's what it means to be a spiritual self-starter. The man who sets his heart to study the Scriptures does not have spiritual anorexia. The man who desires to apply the Scriptures to his life does not have spiritual bulimia.

The Oat Bran Alternative to Anorexia and Bulimia

Psalm 1 deals with the issue of spiritual anorexia. This first psalm contains two key verses pertinent to our discussion. Let's note verse two: *"But his delight is in the law of the LORD, and on his law he meditates day and night."*

Psalm 1 contrasts the righteous man with the wicked man. One key characteristic of the righteous man is that he delights in the law of the Lord. The phrase "law of the Lord" is a synonym for the entire written revelation of God. The word *law* basically means "direction" or "instruction."[3]

The righteous man is not anorexic. He delights in getting clear direction from the Word of God, and this divine direction gives him satisfaction.

The key word in this verse is "meditates." Warren Wiersbe says that meditation is to the soul what digestion is to the body. That is, meditation is spiritual digestion. If a man is either anorexic or bulimic, he will not meditate. And that means he receives none of Scripture's nourishment.

Meditation requires reading, but it is possible to read without meditating. The emphasis here is to read with understanding, to ponder the significance of what God says in His Word. Such a man understands that the Scriptures are his source of spiritual instruction and nutrition, chock-full of spiritual vitamins and minerals. He knows it's his *only* source of spiritual nutrition. The Bible is the meat and potatoes of our spiritual life.

The Christian view of meditation is exactly the reverse of its Eastern rival. In the Eastern version, you empty your mind by chanting some meaningless syllable; in the Christian practice, you fill it with the truth of God's Word in order to ponder the biblical ramifications for your life.

Over one hundred years ago, George Mueller described the benefits of Christian meditation. Read this lengthy quote slowly and carefully to get the full significance of Mueller's wisdom:

I saw more clearly than ever, that the first great and primary business to which I ought to attend every day was to have my soul happy in the Lord. The first thing to be concerned about was not how much I might serve the Lord, how I might glorify the Lord; but how I might get my soul into a happy state, and *how my inner man might be nourished* . . . Now I saw that the most important thing I had to do was to give myself to the reading of the Word of God and to meditation on it, that thus my heart might be comforted, encouraged, warned, reproved, instructed; and that thus, whilst meditating, my heart might be brought into experimental communion with the Lord. I began, therefore, to meditate on the New Testament, from the beginning, early in the morning . . . for the sake of obtaining food for my own soul. And yet now, since God has taught me this point, it is as plain to me as anything, that the first thing a child of God has to do morning by morning is to obtain food for his inner man.

As the outward man is not fit for work for any length of time, except we take food, and as this is one of the first things we do in the morning, so it should be with the inner man . . . Now what is the food for the inner man: not prayer, but the Word of God: and here again not the simple reading of the Word of God, so that it only passes through our minds, just as water runs through a pipe, but considering what we read, pondering over it, and applying it to our hearts. . . .[4]

The antidote for spiritual anorexia and bulimia is scriptural meditation. Meditation enables us to digest the truth of God's Word. A superficial, quick reading of Scripture doesn't cut it. To use Mueller's phrase, that's no different than water running through a pipe.

Are you feeling overwhelmed and discouraged in your walk with Christ? Are you defeated and spiritually ineffective? Have you lost your excitement and enthusiasm in following hard after Christ? Have you so given in to habitual sin that it now threatens to sink you? Have you been duped by the enemy into ignoring the Scripture? Has your schedule become so crowded that you haven't picked up your Bible in weeks? As you step on the spiritual scales, do you find yourself weighing in at less than half of your normal weight? If so, you have been conned into living as though you can survive without the Bible. The result is defeat and malnourishment.

My friend, you cannot live without the Bible. It is your life.

Don't lose heart! There is a way to turn it around, but you will not do so until you grasp several facts. To become a spiritual self-starter, you must develop a personal plan for spiritual growth. That's what this chapter and the next are all about. These two chapters go together. They are a unit. I'll fill in some blanks in the next chapter that I'll leave empty in this one. So stay with me.

Where do you start? Let me offer several suggestions that others have found workable. Ponder these carefully and then pick one or more that could work well for you. Each of them has the same objective: To give you time to interact with the Word and therefore enjoy a nourishing intake of divine wisdom.

1. *Read through the Bible in one year.*

Some of you may have tried this. Perhaps you started well in Genesis, made it through Exodus, and died a slow death in Leviticus. Several guides are available to keep this from happening. I have been reading the Bible through every year for several years.

If this is of interest to you, I recommend you get *The One Year Bible*, published by Tyndale House. This work enables you to get through the entire Bible in one year. The text is divided into daily readings. Each day you read a section from the Old Testament, the New Testament, and a section each from Psalms and Proverbs. The beauty of this is that you can start on any date and jump right into a systematized approach to the Scripture. I highly recommend it. On the same level are *The Daily Walk Bible* (Tyndale) and *The Narrated Bible* (Harvest House). Both are chock-full of pertinent information that will make your daily time in the Word extremely valuable. Any of these three Bibles will get you through the Scripture in one year and help you to grow. They are available at any Christian bookstore.

2. *Listen to the Bible.*

Some of you have unbelievable commutes. The entire Bible is available on cassette tape from numerous companies. Guys with long commutes can pop in a tape instead of listening to the radio. You can stop the tape at certain points and think about what you are hearing and how you can apply it that day at the office or when you get home. Others can listen on their Walkmans as they are out jogging. It would be relatively easy to get through the entire Bible in a year just by utilizing your commute or workout times.

3. *Start a Scripture memory program.*

One of the best ways to lodge the Scriptures in your mind is the *Topical Memory System*, published by the Navigators. This is a convenient set of small cards with printed verses that you can carry in your wallet or keep on the dash of your car. It comes with a guidebook to get you started. Thousands of men all over the world have used this tremendous tool. It's available in any Christian bookstore.

4. *Get involved in Bible Study Fellowship.*

This solid organization offers classes all over the country. It features a five-year course designed to ground you in the Word of God. Weekly assignments keep you involved in a practical study throughout the week.

5. *Form a small accountability group.*

I've seen guys all over the country do this. An accountability group is simply a small group of guys who get together either every week or every two weeks for breakfast or lunch. It can be two guys or five guys—but not much more than that.

The purpose is simply to get together and check in with each other. There is really no agenda other than being honest. The discussion should center around each man giving a report on his spiritual disciplines, his job, his family, and anything else the other men should know about. If you had a rough time with temptation, you should clue them in. If you are facing a personal crisis at home or on the job, you should let them in on it and seek their counsel and prayers.

Obviously, these are men that you know and trust. Everything is confidential. The value of such a group is that it will sharpen you as a spiritual leader of your home. "As iron sharpens iron, so one man sharpens another" (Proverbs 27:17).

I know a group of guys who decided to meet for breakfast just one time to try this. Four years later, they're still meeting every week. Find a good friend and go for it.

The Benefits of Scriptural Meditation

Tremendous personal benefits come from the practice of Scriptural meditation. When you took your current job, undoubtedly one of the things you looked at closely was the benefit package. The benefit package of Psalm 1 is incomparable.

The package, offered to men who meditate on God's Word, is described in verse three: "And he will be like a tree firmly planted by streams of water, which yields its fruit in its season, and its leaf does not wither; and in whatever he does, he prospers" (NASB).

The man who meditates on the Word of God is like a mature, magnificent tree. Such a tree is not only impressive in strength, it's also a thing of beauty. The next time you get an opportunity, go outside and walk around the block. Look for the largest tree on your street, and then take a few minutes to scope it out in detail.

A fully developed oak tree is a magnificent specimen of God's creation. We are impressed with its commanding and imposing presence. That describes precisely the man who has his roots sunk deep into the truth of God's Word.

Did you know that the most critical part of a tree is its root system? Though many folks believe "a tree's spreading superstructure is matched by its underpinnings, in fact the two are not mirror images; the roots may run out as far as three times the crown . . . A typical 40 foot tall tree every day takes in 50 gallons of dissolved nutrients from the soil."[5]

We can only look at the part of the tree that is above the ground. But the amazing thing about such a tree is what is underground. The reason such a tree is so large and impressive is the width and breadth of its root system.

That's precisely the point the writer makes in Psalm 1. A man who wants to be spiritually mature must put his roots deep in the Word of God. Growth comes no other way. No wonder the enemy tries to keep us from the Word.

I grew up in a home with an oak tree right in the middle of the house. It wasn't a red oak, a black oak, or even a white oak. It's the kind of oak described in Isaiah 61:3, and it's called an oak of righteousness. I'm referring to my dad.

Please note that I didn't call him an oak of perfection. But in my opinion, he is an oak of righteousness. I've watched my dad now for forty years. He has never been in full-time ministry. He was and is a businessman. I've seen my dad weather some tough storms. Those of you in real estate know that it tends to be feast or famine.

When my dad was in his early forties, he lost everything. Wiped out financially, he had to start all over—with three boys ready to enter college. It's one thing to be at square one when you're twenty-one; it's quite another when you're forty-three.

I watched him as he saw everything he had collapse. He went from having assets to having nothing but liabilities. He went from a new, spacious home to a small apartment. He literally went from a Cadillac to a Volkswagen. He went from being near the top of the ladder to the bottom.

That's hard on a man. Every day when my dad got up, misery and disappointment were waiting for him. Most of us deal with fear of failure, but my dad actually experienced business failure. I'm sure he was embarrassed and humiliated. That's how I would have felt. Some of you reading this know exactly what that feels like, because you are currently going through similar circumstances.

But you should know something about this catastrophe. My dad never stopped being an oak. Oaks can withstand storms that uproot other trees because of their root system. That perfectly describes my dad.

The great fighter Joe Louis once said, "I don't like money actually, but it quiets my nerves." But what do you do when the money isn't there? How do you quiet your nerves when one look at your checkbook opens the acid valve to your stomach?

For as long as I've known my dad, he has gotten up early. He gets up around 5:45 to meet with the Lord. That's a standing appointment he's kept every day for more than forty years. The very first thing my dad does each morning is to pick up his Bible, worn and used, its margins full of notes and its pages frayed.

I can remember several times as a little boy waking up early and going into the living room to see my dad kneeling in front of the couch with his Bible open in front of him. While it was still dark, he was taking in his fifty gallons of nutrients from the soil of God's Word.

That's why my dad is an oak. He's been a spiritual self-starter for a long time. He is a man who has meditated and digested the Word of God every day of his adult life. His root system goes deep into the Scriptures. And that's what enabled him to withstand his storm of twenty-some years ago. He stood tall and survived because he has a mighty root system.

My dad knows I'm writing this book, but he doesn't know I'm writing this about him. If he saw what I was writing, he wouldn't be too comfortable. He wouldn't object because I mentioned his business failure, but he would say that I am making him look too good. I'm not. But that is why my dad won't see this until he gets the first copy to come off the press.

I've written about him for four reasons. First, because it was a privilege to grow up in a home with an oak of righteousness. Some people in the Midwest have never seen the ocean. Others have never seen a giant redwood. Still others, no doubt, have never seen an oak of righteousness. I was raised by one.

Second, I'm writing about my dad because I saw that the secret to surviving the storms of life is to have a large tap root that goes deep into the Scriptures. My dad's business may have been failing, but his leadership at home was never stronger than during this tough time. As a result, our family was never more secure or stable than it was during this difficult season. The test of leadership is crisis. My dad passed the test because he checked the field manual every day.

Third, I know that some of you right now are in the biggest storm of your lives. I have written this to encourage you to get your roots deep into the Bible. That's what will keep you strong and steady in the storm. The Lord is not trying to ruin you, He is only rebuilding you. But you must digest His Word to stay strong. Don't lose heart. You *will* make it because Christ is with you. He still knows how to calm the storm. At the right time, He'll calm your storm, too.

Fourth, I have written about my dad because none of us know what the future holds. None of us are financially secure, although we may think we are. None of us are emotionally secure, although up to now we may have been. None of us have a guarantee of health, although we tend to think we do. Consciously or subconsciously, we think we are exempt from certain hardships in life because to this point in life we've escaped them. But there are no guarantees.

Anne Morrow Lindbergh once said, "Only when a tree has fallen can you take the measure of it. It is the same with a man." I found that to be true with my dad. When he fell financially, it became clear to everyone that he was a very, very big tree.

Twenty-five years later, God has given it all back to him. God has restored the years the locusts have eaten. My dad is now in pretty fair shape financially because of the Lord's faithfulness. He certainly isn't wealthy, but he's comfortable. But I'll tell you this. He could lose it all tomorrow at the age of sixty-seven and have to start all over again. I honestly don't think it would shake him. The roots are just too deep. And when the roots are that deep, it has a way of quieting the nerves.

CHAPTER SIX

Aerobic Kneeling

*In these days of exceptional evil,
are you doing something exceptional?*
Dr. Martyn Lloyd-Jones

Yogi Berra was catching for the Yankees, and his team was on a road trip. One night, Yogi got hungry for a pizza. He called a local pizza joint and ordered a medium pepperoni. When he walked up to the counter to pick it up, the man said, "Yogi, when you called, I forgot to ask how you wanted me to slice your medium pepperoni. Do you want it cut into six slices or twelve?"

Yogi thought about it. "Better make it six," he said, "I don't think I can eat twelve."

Our discussion on becoming a spiritual self-starter could be compared to a pizza. Only this pizza you cut in half. There are two parts to becoming a spiritual self-starter. The previous chapter covered the first half. This one has the second.

In this chapter, I'm making three assumptions. Without understanding the assumptions, nothing else in this section will make sense.

- Assumption #1: *The Christian life is not a 100-yard dash. It is a marathon.*

- Assumption #2: *In the Christian life, it's not how you start, it's how you finish.*

- Assumption #3: *Spiritual self-starters train aerobically.*

Men who want to lead their families effectively must become spiritual self-starters. We covered the first minimum requirement for being a spiritual self-starter—meditating on Scripture—in the last chapter. Now it's time for the second.

An Effective Training Program

Have you ever noticed how often the New Testament refers to exercise? For instance:

Therefore, since we have so great a cloud of witnesses surrounding us, let us also lay aside every encumbrance, and the sin which so easily entangles us, *and let us run with endurance the race that is set before us* (Hebrews 12:1, NASB).

Have nothing to do with godless myths and old wives' tales; rather, *train yourself to be godly.* For physical training is of some value,

134

but godliness has value for all things, holding promise for both the present life and the life to come (1 Timothy 4:7-8).

The first passage insists that endurance is needed to run the race of the Christian life. You don't need endurance to run one hundred yards. You do, however, need endurance to run 26 miles, 385 yards. Endurance is necessary if you are going to finish. That's why there are no starting blocks in the Christian life. Marathoners don't need starting blocks. When you're running a marathon, your focus isn't on your start—it's on your finish.

It's like the story Steve Brown tells about two men walking in the woods who suddenly hear the roar of a grizzly bear. Both men know what grizzlies can do, and one of the men immediately sits down to put on his running shoes. His companion blurts out, "You don't really think you're going to outrun that bear, do you?"

"Of course I'm not going to outrun that bear," the man replies. "I don't have to. I just have to outrun *you*."

The point is this: Your level of endurance is important. In the Christian life, it's not how you start, it's how you finish. This entire chapter on aerobic kneeling is about endurance: What it is, how one develops it, and the phenomenal benefits it brings.

The passage from 1 Timothy gives the secret of obtaining endurance. It's called training. Recently I was watching the late edition of SportsCenter on ESPN to catch highlights of that day's NFL games. After football, they showed about a twenty-second clip of the New York marathon. It was incredible to watch nearly twenty thousand people in one race. I don't know how many finished, but I'd bet you a used piece of gum that every person who did had something in common with every other finisher. What could ten or twelve thousand runners of different races, professions, and income levels all have in common?

They trained.

If you're like me, you're concerned about staying in shape. I think men can be divided into two groups: Those who exercise, and those who feel guilty when they don't. None of us are interested in keeling over from a heart attack at forty-five. I know I'm not real excited about the possibility of going under the knife for a triple bypass. So we exercise to stay in shape.

Dr. Kenneth Cooper, founder of the Aerobics Institute, knows what it means to be in shape:

> Passive fitness, the mere absence of any illness, is a losing battle. Without activity, the body begins to deteriorate and appears to become more vulnerable to certain chronic illnesses and diseases. Muscular fitness is of some value, but it too is limited. It concentrates on only one system in the body, one of the least important ones, and has limited beneficial effect on the essential organs or overall health. It's like putting a lovely new coat of paint on an automobile that really needs a new engine overhaul. *Endurance fitness should be your goal. It will ensure all the benefits of the training effect, improving not just your muscles, but your lungs, your heart, and your blood vessels. It is the foundation on which all forms of fitness should be built.*[1]

Cooper says the key to endurance training is oxygen consumption. The body needs oxygen to produce energy. Cooper refers to the "training effect." The training effect is the whole goal of endurance exercise. Jogging for five minutes will have little effect on your heart and legs. Getting in your car and driving three miles instead of running will have no effect. But if you jog between thirty and forty-five minutes, you will definitely have a positive effect on your heart and lungs.

This is why we run, swim, or play full-court basketball for a couple of hours. Some even dance. But it has to be aerobic dancing. (Usually, real men don't do aerobic dancing. Their wives do. Real men only slow dance. With their own wives.)

Let me ask you a serious question. How do you stay in shape spiritually? If you are going to run the race with endurance and train yourself for godliness, what kind of exercises do you do? In the physical realm you can do aerobic jogging, aerobic basketball, aerobic swimming, aerobic cycling, etc. But in the spiritual realm there is only one such exercise. It's what I call aerobic kneeling.

It's also known as prayer.

Prayer is to the soul what exercise is to the body. A spiritual self-starter is a man who is in good spiritual shape. That means he does two things: (1) He consistently eats the nutritious diet of the Scriptures; and (2) he consistently spends time in aerobic kneeling. *Prayer is the exercise of the man who is a spiritual self-starter.*

These two elements must go together. A marathon runner not only trains efficiently but eats correctly. Both enable him to have physical endurance. The same is true in the Christian life.

There are two mistakes we can make in our desire to be spiritual self-starters:

- Emphasize Scripture without prayer;
- Emphasize prayer without Scripture.

We need both the right diet and the right exercise. Prayer and Scripture go together, and we are most effective when we have a good balance of the two. The man who studies the Bible without praying will develop a good mind with a cold heart. The man who prays without knowing Scripture will consistently pray outside the will of God, for that is where His will is revealed. This balance is critical to standing firm in spiritual battle. Paul could not have made it any clearer in Ephesians 6:17-18:

> And [take] the sword of the Spirit, which is the word of God. *With all prayer and petition . . .* (NASB).

Have you seen the Latin phrase *sine qua non*? Literally, it means "without which, nothing." It fits here. Without a diet of Scripture and an exercise routine of prayer, you've got nothing. You can't finish the Christian marathon without them. In fact, you can't even begin.

How to Develop Spiritual Endurance

The natural question at this point is, "How often does one have to exercise aerobic kneeling to stay in good spiritual condition?"

Before I answer, you should know something about me. I'm a jogger. I've marked out a three-mile course in my neighborhood that I cover *every* day. No exceptions. Snow, ice, hurricanes, earthquakes, or tornadoes cannot keep me from this discipline. This three-mile course is such a priority in my life that even if I don't have time to run, I'll get in the car and drive it.

I have a friend who is also a jogger. We are in the same church, approximately the same age, and both wear the same brand of running shoe. Yet he intimidates me to the point of embarrassment. The farthest I have ever run in my life without stopping is four miles. I have never run a 10K, much less a marathon.

My friend doesn't run marathons, either. He likes to run *ultra*-marathons. His races aren't twenty-six miles long, but one hundred. I can't *drive* a hundred miles without stopping.

This guy appears to be normal. He has a successful medical practice, a lovely wife, and two fine boys. But I have reached the conclusion he is not normal. He is abnormal, and the *American Heritage Dictionary* backs me up. It says the word normal means "conforming to a usual or typical pattern." He certainly does not conform to the usual or typical pattern in regard to running. That's why he's abnormal in this area.

Hundreds of thousands of joggers in this country consistently run twelve to eighteen miles a week. I'm in that group and so are many of you. Out of that group, a good sized percentage have entered a 10K race. A much smaller percentage of those have finished a marathon. But how many out of all the runners across the United States have ever finished a one hundred mile race? Probably less than 1 percent. Why? Because the other 99 percent are normal. The ultra-marathoners are nuts, and everybody knows it. Yet here I am, feeling intimidated by some guy who is abnormal!

I've talked with my friend about physical exercise because he's a doctor. He makes it clear to all his patients they should have a goal to be in good physical condition. Yet he doesn't recommend that any of his patients follow his running schedule. Why? Because it isn't necessary to run like that to stay in shape. In fact, he recommends the same thing that Dr. Cooper does. According to Dr. Cooper, a jogger only needs to run for thirty minutes, three or four times a week, to be in top cardiovascular condition. This, of course, assumes his workout is rigorous enough to adequately exercise his heart according to the aerobic point system. But that's all it takes! Three times a week for thirty minutes at a clip. That's only ninety minutes out of a seven-day week.

According to that standard, there are multitudes of runners who couldn't run an ultra-marathon but who nevertheless are in excellent physical condition!

Now let's get back to the original question: *How often does one have to exercise aerobic kneeling to stay in good spiritual shape?* The Bible is surprisingly silent about the amount of time one should spend in prayer. It emphasizes prayer without telling how much time to give to prayer.

I know what you're thinking. *Doesn't Paul say somewhere* (1 Thessalonians 5:17, NASB) *to "pray without ceasing"?* Yes, he does. But Paul, in that passage, is describing an attitude of life, not a life devoted exclusively to praying.

There is no passage in the New Testament that tells me I should spend X amount of time in prayer every day. There is no inspired prescription about the time requirements necessary for prayer. That means I have to figure it out for myself. I've examined quite a few books on prayer in order to get some insight into this question. Here's what I've come up with.

Most books on prayer will cite person after person—usually some great missionary or minister from the past—who would spend three to four hours a day in prayer. Book after book holds up these people as the *normal* examples. For instance, one writer says: "Bishop Ken was so much with God that his soul was said to be God-enamored. He was with God before the clock struck three every morning. Bishop Asbury said: 'I propose to rise at four o'clock as often as I can and spend two hours in prayer and meditation.' Samuel Rutherford . . . rose at three in the morning to meet God in prayer. Joseph Alleine arose at four o'clock for his business of praying till eight . . . John Welch, the holy and wonderful Scotch preacher, thought the day ill spent if he did not spend eight to ten hours in prayer."[2]

I don't know about you, but the only time I get up at three in the morning is when I've got a sinus infection (and I'm not getting up to pray about it; I'm getting up to breathe). The last time I got up at 4 A.M. was to go deep sea fishing.

These guys were unbelievable! Can you imagine spending two to four hours a day in prayer? I know a lot of guys who spend two to four hours commuting, but not too many who spend that much time praying. Is that what God expects of you and me?

No wonder most of us feel guilty about our prayer lives! Did any of these guys ever sleep? Books always point out what time they got up, but when did they go to bed? They sure didn't stay up to watch "The Tonight Show." These guys intimidate the socks off me. They intimidate me in the same way spiritually that my ultra-marathoner buddy intimidates me physically.

Please don't misunderstand. I admire each one of these men. They were greatly used of God. Many of them were used to open entire nations to the gospel. But that's the point. With great respect, I suggest they were *abnormal,* for they do not conform to the usual or typical pattern. They each had abnormal and extraordinary spiritual responsibilities that called for remarkable measures in prayer. Because of their exceptional responsibilities for churches, missions organizations, and even nations, they trained themselves to become ultra-marathoners in prayer.

I respectfully suggest that they are no more the norm for prayer than an Olympic medal winner in the marathon is the norm for joggers. Very few men are cut out to be ultra-marathoners, whether in running or praying. Of all the millions of Christians who have followed Christ over the last two thousand years, probably less than one-half of one percent prayed two to four hours every day. That is not to be the pattern for prayer any more than running one hundred miles is the norm for jogging. I don't believe you have to pray two to fours hours a day to be in shape spiritually. I don't believe you have to get up at three o'clock every morning to lead your family through the moral chaos of the 1990s.

So how much time should we give to aerobic kneeling?

Consider with me an idea I've been chewing on

for awhile. If exercise in the physical realm requires thirty minutes, three times a week, then why not apply that same principle to the spiritual? I realize Kenneth Cooper didn't get aerobics from the New Testament, and I'm not suggesting my idea has any scriptural basis. It's only an observation from the physical that may have application to the spiritual.

If thirty minutes, three times a week, provides the necessary endurance for the physical, then would it be off-base to suggest the same schedule might give me endurance for the spiritual life? I don't think so. Especially for the man who currently isn't exercising at all.

If something is important to us, we usually can find three or four thirty-minute segments in our schedules each week to accomplish it. Let's say you decided to shoot for this goal. If you did it three times a week, in a year's time, you would have spent approximately seventy-eight hours in one-on-one time with the Lord. If you had four thirty-minute appointments annually, that would give you one hundred and four hours. Seventy-eight or more hours in a year with the Lord in concentrated, one-on-one time is nothing to feel guilty about.

Hundreds of thousands of people spend that much time jogging every year. Many of you devote that much time to physical exercise. I commend you for making wise use of your time. However, the Scripture is clear when it says ". . . train yourself to be godly. For physical training is of some value, but godliness has value for all things, holding promise for both the present life and the life to come" (1 Timothy 4:7-8).

Paul didn't say physical exercise has no benefit; he said it is of *limited* benefit. On the other hand, spiritual exercise—the pursuit of God—has immense profit because it pays dividends now as well as in eternity. You do well to exercise your body, but the priority in your life should be spiritual exercise. Too many of us have these priorities reversed.

Chuck Colson is razor sharp when he asks: "If there are so many Christians in the U.S., why aren't we affecting our world? . . . We treat our faith like a section of the newspaper or an item on our 'Things to Do Today' list. We file religion in our schedules between relatives and running. It's just one of the many concerns competing for our attention. Not that we aren't serious about it. We go to church and attend Bible studies. But we're just as serious about our jobs and physical fitness."[3]

As you examine your life, have you made physical exercise a higher priority than spiritual exercise? If you have, you've made the wrong decision. I'm not suggesting you give up physical exercise so that you can spiritually exercise. I am suggesting that you do both, because I think most of us have room in our lives for both. But quite frankly, if you had to decide between the two, physical exercise should come in second.

What do you think would happen if thousands of Christian men got their priorities right and started to get serious about prayer? Do you think it might make a difference in this spiritual battle we're in? Do you think it might make a difference in our ability to lead our families? Do you think it might have an impact on our society if men all over this country began making a commitment to spend time with the Lord in meditation and prayer?

I am not talking about an unrealistic, impractical approach to prayer. I am talking about an approach that is realistic, practical, and achievable for almost anyone who takes seriously the responsibility to spiritually lead his home.

Gentlemen, if we are going to be spiritual leaders for our wives and children, can we opt for anything less? We need to make time to soak ourselves in God's Word; we need time to chew on what the Scripture is saying to us; we need time to come before God and ask Him to give us the wisdom we need to be His men in this world.

We need to come before Him and ask for His wisdom as we make daily decisions at work and at home. We need to pray for our marriages, that we might be protected from the assaults of the evil one. We need to pray for our children that God would draw them to Christ, that He would keep us in tune with them and their needs, that He would enable them to be strong to withstand the pressure that comes from their peers. We need to remember in times of stress and hardship that "the angel of the LORD encamps around those who fear him, and he delivers them" (Psalm 34:7). I need time with the Lord to remind me that it's not my private battle, it's His.

The tragedy is that many fine Christian men openly confess that prayer is not a priority. If the truth were known, we would find that many of us go *weeks* without spending time in scriptural meditation and prayer. No wonder we feel defeated and over-whelmed! We have no spiritual energy or power. We have no spiritual endurance. This is why we so easily cave in to temptation. We have nothing to fight with. Our Bibles are gathering dust ("Honey, have you seen my Bible?") and our prayer lives consist of mumbled petitions before dinner. If that is your spiritual condition, you are no match for the assaults of the enemy.

My friend, you have to get in shape. You must "train yourself for godliness." And you can.

Recognize up front, however, that five-minute quiet times will not prepare you for the battle ahead. Let's be honest. If five minutes of jogging won't bring about physical endurance, then why would five minutes of prayer and Bible reading provide spiritual endurance? Yet the enemy will try to convince you that it's enough. Listen to Dr. Martyn Lloyd-Jones:

> If he [Satan] causes us to neglect the reading and studying of the Word, and the understanding of the Word, it will suit him admirably. If he causes us to neglect praying we shall faint, and in that condition become an easy and obvious prey . . . if you really believe that just to read a few verses and a short comment on them in a matter of five minutes, and to have a brief word of prayer, is adequate for your day, then I say that you do not know anything about the wiles of the devil. That is not the New Testament; that has not been the verdict of the saints throughout the centuries. But a superficial spirituality imagines that is enough—"I have . . . had my quiet time"—not aware of any stagnation in the soul, not aware of a lack of growth, not aware of an appalling superficiality.[4]

So where do you start? What if you really aren't spending any time with the Lord? Where do you begin?

What's the first step? How do you begin to get yourself in spiritual shape? Let me suggest a plan workable for anyone reading these pages.

A Plan for Aerobic Spiritual Fitness

As I lay out this plan, I'm going to assume you are not spending *any* time during a given week with the Lord. I know that many of you are, but for the purpose of explaining this plan, I need to start at square one.

The key word in developing these two spiritual disciplines is PLAN. As David Campbell has said, "If you don't know where you're going, you'll probably end up somewhere else." I remember years ago trying to get started with personal prayer and Bible study. But after a few days or weeks, I would fizzle. It wasn't until I got a plan that I started to enjoy some success.

Every year, thousands of people attend the Super Bowl. Do they just wake up on Saturday morning, read about the Super Bowl taking place the next day in New Orleans or wherever, and impulsively decide to hop on a plane and go to the game? Of course not. Attending a Super Bowl requires planning that begins months in advance.

When you get your paycheck, do you just go down to the bank, cash it, and carry a roll of bills in your pocket all month? Of course not. You have planned beforehand how that paycheck is to be distributed. A budget is a planned expenditure of money. That's why it's a wise move to meet with a financial planner.

We plan everything in our lives that's worth doing. We plan to take trips, establish budgets, invite friends to parties, take the car in for tune-ups, get an annual physical examination, and write weekly grocery lists. Everything that is important we plan. And that is precisely why most of us don't pray. *We simply don't plan to pray.* It's not that we don't want to or intend to. It's not an issue of desire. It's an issue of planning. Because we haven't planned to pray, somehow we never quite get around to it.

I believe there are four necessary components in an effective plan for aerobic kneeling.

1. *Plan a time.*

A good rule of thumb is to begin your day by meeting with the Lord. Not everyone's schedule allows for this. But if possible, plan to have a morning briefing with the Lord. John Piper is right: "Where a man belongs is up early and alone with God seeking vision and direction for his family."[5]

As I mentioned before, my dad has had a standing appointment with the Lord every morning at 5:45 for over forty years. He planned to pray. He made it a priority. And God has honored him for it.

As you look at your schedule, what time will work for you?

2. *Plan a place.*

We are constantly planning places. We plan places to live, to have lunch, to play racquetball, and to have tailgate parties. Whenever you make an appointment, you plan a place to meet.

The same is true with prayer. It could be your den, your office, or your bedroom. The only criteria is that it needs to be a place where you can have some privacy and not be disturbed.

I have a friend who has such a long commute to work that it's impossible for him to have time with the Lord first thing in the morning. So he takes four lunch hours a week and spends those with the Lord. He simply shuts the door, tells his secretary he's not taking any calls, and meets with the Lord. His office is his place. What's going to be yours?

3. *Make a list.*

Write down the people and issues you want to pray about. I have a list I carry in my Daytimer. I have a daily section, under which I include the things I need to pray for each day. Other items are listed under different days of the week. On Tuesday I pray for my extended family. I pray for my wife and kids every day, but on Tuesday I include aunts, uncles, brothers, parents, cousins, etc. I use Thursday to pray for my colleagues in ministry around the country, guys I know who carry large ministry responsibilities. When I run into one of them, I can truthfully say I pray for him once a week.

What should you put on your list? Anything. God is interested in every aspect of your life. Pray for your wife, your kids, your pastor, your elders and deacons. Pray for this country that God would begin to turn it around spiritually. Pray for the president, your congressional representatives, and the Supreme Court justices as they make critical decisions.

As you work your way through your list, it's a good idea to pray specifically instead of generally. Instead of saying, "Lord, bless my children today" say, "Lord, give each of my children wisdom today to stand for what is right instead of giving in to peer pressure." "Lord, please give their teachers wisdom in understanding my children as they teach them today." You never know when a general prayer is answered, but specific prayers are answered specifically.

4. *Begin with Scripture.*

This is where our discussion in the last chapter comes in. I've been told that for years Billy Graham has read five psalms and one chapter of Proverbs each morning. There are 150 psalms and thirty-one chapters in Proverbs, so that will put you through both books twelve times a year.

Another suggestion made earlier is to read through the entire Bible each year. I usually begin by reading a portion of Scripture that I'm working through. That helps me to warm up to prayer. *There is no magic formula!* Keep at it, and you will find what works best for you.

Private time with the Lord in prayer and Scripture will yield tremendous benefits. Approximately fifteen minutes in the Scripture and fifteen minutes in prayer three times a week will keep you aerobically fit. That's something any of us can do. (Of course, if you are reading through the Bible in one year, you'll have to read daily to keep pace.)

Find a time, find a place, and make it a habit. That's all spiritual disciplines are: Cultivated habits. Horace Mann once observed: "Habit is a cable; we weave a thread of it each day, and at last we cannot break it." Give yourself six weeks with a certain time in a certain place with a certain list, and you will be well on your way to establishing a systematic habit.

A fifth item concludes my suggestions.

5. *Make yourself accountable to someone.*

Why would you need to do this? Because you need at least two or three people to provide encouragement as you begin this new discipline. It's critical. Sharing your personal commitment to pray three times a week with your wife or a good friend can come in handy when you start to fall back on your commitment. If someone has the freedom to ask you every couple of weeks about your progress, you will be motivated to follow through . . . even when you don't feel like it.

Chuck Swindoll offers insight for living when he writes:

> Being creatures with blind spots and tendencies toward rationalization, we must also be in close touch with a few trustworthy individuals with whom we meet on a regular basis. Knowing that such an encounter is going to happen helps us hold the line morally and ethically. I know of nothing more effective for maintaining a pure heart and keeping one's life balanced and on target than being a part of an accountability group. It is amazing what such a group can provide to help us hold our passions in check!

> Recently, I was encouraged to hear about a minister who meets once a week with a small group of men. They are committed to one another's purity. They pray with and for each other. They talk openly and honestly about their struggles, weaknesses, temptations, and trials. In addition to these general things, they look one another in the eye as they ask and answer no less than seven specific questions:

1. Have you been with a woman this week in such a way that was inappropriate or could have looked to others that you were using poor judgment?

2. Have you been completely above reproach in all your financial dealings this week?

3. Have you exposed yourself to any explicit material this week?

4. Have you spent daily time in prayer and in the Scriptures this week?

5. Have you fulfilled the mandate of your calling this week?

6. Have you taken time off to be with your family this week?

7. Have you just lied to me?[6]

The High Hurdles of Aerobic Kneeling

Aerobic kneeling comes under the category of spiritual discipline. It takes time to develop any kind of discipline. As you attempt to pray, you will encounter boredom, frustration, and monotony. As you attempt to develop these disciplines, you will encounter resistance. Let me list several high hurdles I frequently confront in prayer:

- My mind wanders.

- I run out of things to say.

- I'll be praying about something and suddenly remember I forgot to return an important call yesterday afternoon.

- I say stupid things I don't really mean.
- I get bored.

What do you do when you find your mind wandering? I simply say, "Lord, excuse me. My mind got off the track somehow. Help me to keep focused this morning." Prayer is a developed discipline. We cannot call an 800 number and have discipline shipped to us overnight by Federal Express.

If you are going to run the race with endurance, you must develop habits that will enable you to spend at least thirty minutes with the Lord, three or four times a week. That's within anyone's reach. If you are doing that, you don't need to feel guilty about prayer and Bible study.

I know some will disagree. They insist that it must be done every day. That is the ideal, and I agree. But before you can run an ultra-marathon, you have to make it around the track once. Before you run a marathon, you need to finish a 10K. Before you try to run one hundred miles, make sure you can finish twenty-six.

It takes time to develop a prayer life. But three or four times a week, consistently, will keep you in good shape spiritually. That is training yourself for godliness. As you mature, you can increase the frequency of your spiritual exercise. And as the years go by, God will have raised up some men to become the next generation of marathoners and ultra-marathoners.

Gentlemen, if we are to lead our families, we have to get in shape. Time in prayer and Bible study doesn't come easily. You are in for the fight of your life if you decide to go for it. Our microwave culture offers instant oatmeal and instant coffee, but the

Christian life has no microwaves. In the Christian life, you have to wait for the oatmeal and you have to wait for the coffee. You have to wait to develop endurance and godliness. It is going to take time, lots of time. But it is well worth the effort. George McCluskey would vouch for that.

You've probably never heard of George McCluskey. To my knowledge, no biographies have been written about his life. McCluskey was a man who decided to make a shrewd investment. As he married and started a family, he decided to invest one hour a day in prayer. He was concerned that his kids might follow Christ and establish their own homes where Christ was honored. After a time, he decided to expand his prayers to include not only his children, but their children and the children after them. Every day between 11 A.M. and noon, he would pray for the next three generations.

As the years went by, his two daughters committed their lives to Christ and married men who went into full-time ministry. The two couples produced four girls and one boy. Each of the girls married a minister and the boy became a pastor. The first two children born to this generation were both boys. Upon graduation from high school, the two cousins chose the same college and became roommates. During their sophomore year, one of the boys decided to go into the ministry as well. The other one didn't. He knew the family history and undoubtedly felt some pressure to continue the family legacy by going into the ministry himself, but he chose not to. In a manner of speaking, this young man became the black sheep of the family. He was the first one in four generations not to go into full-time Christian ministry.

He decided to pursue his interest in psychology and, over the years, met with success. After earning his doctorate, he wrote a book to parents that became a best-seller. He then wrote another and another, all best-sellers. Eventually he started a radio program that is now heard on more than a thousand stations each day. The black sheep's name? James Dobson, without a doubt the most influential and significant leader of the pro-family movement in America. His ministry is the direct result of the prayers of a man who lived four generations ago.

I don't know about you, but my family could sure use a black sheep like that.

CHAPTER SEVEN

Husband and Wife Teamwork in the Marriage Cockpit

Two are better than one, because they have a good return for their work: If one falls down, his friend can help him up. But pity the man who falls and has no one to help him up!
Ecclesiastes 4:9-10

I do a fair amount of flying. That's why I almost had a coronary when I read a *Readers Digest* report on the crash of Continental flight 1713.

It had been snowing hard in Denver on the day of the crash. That's nothing unusual in Colorado. But a number of other things were unusual.

According to the magazine, "United Airlines, the other major carrier operating out of Denver, had canceled its Boise flights because of the storm."[1] Due to the United cancellations, Continental flight 1713 was almost full. Undoubtably, some of the passengers thought it unusual for one airline to cancel flights while another kept flying. But due to a myriad unknown reasons, seventy-seven people boarded the plane despite the severe weather.

Something else was highly unusual. One of the experienced flight attendants was concerned about the cockpit crew. "In an extraordinary step, she took Capt. Frank Zvonek aside at the gate and questioned him about the proficiency of the first officer. The man's extremely youthful appearance worried her."[2]

Her instincts, unfortunately, were on target. "He was Lee Bruecher, 26, and in fact had completed his DC-9 flight training only eight weeks earlier and had hardly flown since. Before joining Continental, he had been fired from another job for his incompetence as a pilot . . . Captain Zvonek told Kelly not to worry. He assured her that he would not let Bruecher land the plane on their return flight to Denver later that day. The prospect of the captain's letting the young first officer be at the controls during takeoff was so unthinkable to Kelly that it did not even occur to her to ask *that* question."

Yet the unusual continued to happen. "As the DC-9 jetliner prepared for its roll down the runway . . . The captain was not at the controls. Instead, he had delegated primary flying duties to First Officer Lee Bruecher. In addition to his dismal record with small commercial aircraft, Bruecher had spent only 36 hours in his whole life flying big commercial jet aircraft. And Frank Zvonek himself, the commander who had turned the controls over to Bruecher, had only 33 hours of experience as DC-9 captain. Neither man had ever flown a DC-9 in weather like this."

But one other irregular circumstance sealed the fate of flight 1713. "Not only are pilots required to visually check the wings every 20 minutes during freezing wet weather, but no more than 20 minutes should elapse between de-icing and takeoff.

"Particles of ice no larger than grains of coarse sandpaper can significantly disrupt the flow of air over the wing surface—a condition that has a critical effect on the plane's ability to lift during takeoff. On this day, 27 minutes had elapsed since flight 1713 was de-iced—seven minutes beyond the maximum time—which gave ample opportunity for ice to form. Neither pilot ever emerged from the cockpit to walk back into the cabin and inspect the wing surfaces."[3]

What were they doing when they should have been checking the wings? According to the article, "The two Continental pilots had never met each other until this flight, but in the cockpit, after completing the standard checklists, they fell into a pattern of aimless chatter with sexual innuendoes about one of the stewardesses. Their last 30 minutes of conversation, saved for posterity by the cockpit voice recorder, are more remindful of two adolescent boys on a camp-out than of two professionals charged with the safety of eighty men, women and children."[4]

The tragic outcome of these unusual circumstances? Flight 1713 crashed just seconds after take off, and twenty-eight people, including Zvonek and Breucher, lost their lives.

You and I both know that competent teamwork in the cockpits of commercial airliners is the norm.

That's why it's safer to fly than it is to drive. Yet this investigative report revealed an exception to that long-standing aviation tradition of teamwork between an experienced captain and copilot.

There's a reason for two pilots up front: Two are better than one. If the captain were to suffer a heart attack at thirty-two thousand feet, the first officer could safely bring the plane in. But there's another reason: One pilot can make a mistake. If one makes a mistake, chances are the other will notice it and correct it.

The mistake made by the captain of flight 1713 in failing to de-ice the plane within the given time limits should have been caught by the first officer. But it wasn't. And lives were lost because of the mutual error. It boiled down to a simple, yet catastrophic, lack of teamwork.

Flying the Marriage 747

Sometimes life reminds me of flying a plane. Not just any plane, but a massive 747. My wife and I are up front in the cockpit. Right behind the cockpit door in first class are our three kids, one great-grandmother, two sets of grandparents, assorted uncles, aunts, cousins, nieces and nephews, and some close friends.

As you go down the spiral staircase, you find all of the other people and things that travel with us through life. You'll find one church, two schools, three school teachers, a piano teacher, a pediatrician, a general practitioner, an allergist, a gynecologist, an orthodontist, an attorney trying to collect from the insurance company that won't pay the bills for my wife's whiplash, an accountant, a soccer team, a basketball team, a baseball team, a group of ten-year-old girls who carpool to a ranch once a week to ride horses, a mechanic who actually fixes my car the first time, a travel agent who books my flights, an insurance agent I've never laid eyes on, a pharmacist who seems to get a tithe of my paycheck each month, and a grocery store that gets the other nine-tenths.

In the cargo area, you'll find an Audi in need of wax, a Chevy Suburban in need of a new transmission, a house soon to get new carpet, a frequently abused budget, a trampoline which doubles as a family room sofa, a dog recovering from a hysterectomy, and a partridge in a pear tree. Sound familiar?

The way I figure it, most families have so much going on that they could easily fill up a 747 with everyone and everything that's a part of their lives.

Donald Trump has his own airline. Every one of his planes carries the name "Trump." It seems to me that most of us have enough action in our own lives to merit at least one 747 with our name emblazoned on the side. Just think of it. The next time you went to the airport you would not only see planes marked Trump, but you'd see Farrar, Brown, Garcia, Nakamura, Johansen, Alms, Wilson, Dabney, and Owens. Those are the family 747s.

You and your wife are up front trying to keep your ship airborne. You're surrounded by gauges, instruments, and lights. Everything is going smoothly . . . when suddenly a red light starts blinking furiously. That particular light indicates your daughter needs braces—with a $3,000 price tag. A quick look at the financial gauge indicates that your "dental" account is close to empty. Your budget allowed for some cleanings and a few cavities, but no braces. Where in the world will that money come from?

As you try to convince yourself that your daughter would look just fine with crooked teeth, the medical light indicates your five-year-old has just picked up mononucleosis from a kid at kindergarten. The pediatrician says that for him to fully recover he is not to run, jump, or play for the next two years. Good luck.

Before you can work out the ramifications of keeping a five-year-old still for two years, an alarm goes off over your head. Your son's favorite summer basketball camp has just raised its one-week fee from $500 to $17,000. The thought of hiring an arsonist to burn it down crosses your mind. But you can't do that. You're a Christian, remember?

Does any of this sound familiar? Of course it does. It's real life. It's tough trying to keep the family 747 in the air. That's why teamwork is as essential in the marriage cockpit as it is in a commercial jetliner.

How tragic that family 747s crash every day simply because husbands and wives have never understood how they are to operate and function *as a team*. On the other hand, a couple that knows and practices the correct procedures greatly increases its chances of marital survival when the family airliner encounters sudden turbulence.

This is a chapter about teamwork in the marriage cockpit. There are three necessary procedures that promote teamwork in the marriage cockpit:

- Mutual understanding of the Montana-Rice principle,
- Mutual accountability,
- Mutual submission.

If you can grab hold of these principles, your

wife will not only appreciate you for it, but the chances of her following your leadership will increase dramatically.

The Montana-Rice Principle

What version of the Bible do you prefer? The NIV, NASB, TLB, or KJV? When it comes to Ephesians 5:22-23, I like the NFL version:

"Wide receivers, submit to your quarterback, as to the Lord. For the quarterback is the head of the wide receiver as Christ is the head of the church . . ."

This verse is the basis for what I call the Montana-Rice principle. San Francisco 49ers Joe Montana and Jerry Rice are one of the most dangerous passing combinations in the history of the National Football League. To watch Montana and Rice operate is sheer bliss. Their ability to work together can shred an entire defense before you get a chance to swallow your Gatorade.

The Montana-Rice principle is made up of two components. Unless they both understood these components, they could not enjoy the success that is theirs nearly every time they step on the field.

Component #1: Joe Montana has authority over Jerry Rice.

Component #2: Jerry is to submit to Joe's authority.

Let's take a look at the significance of these two components. In the huddle, Montana makes the decisions. When the play comes in from the sideline, he's the one who decides whether or not to audibilize when he get to the line of scrimmage and sees the defense.

The reason he can make these decisions is that he is the "head." That means he is the one with "authority." In the huddle, Montana has the final say because he's the quarterback. Everyone on the team knows this. That's why when he audibilizes, Jerry doesn't yell over to Joe and say, "That's the stupidest call I've ever heard in my life." Montana is the head, and he ultimately makes the decisions on the field.

This doesn't mean that Rice is denied critical input to the decisions Montana makes in the huddle. If Rice comes back to the huddle and tells Montana that the cornerback keeps taking his inside move, and that he should fake to the inside and then run a post, Montana's probably going to listen to him. Why? Because they both have the same objective. They want to win.

Rice and the other 49ers on the offensive unit "submit" to Montana's leadership. The word translated "submit" in Ephesians 5:22 means "to line one's self under." It was often used in the military sense of soldiers submitting to their superior. The word primarily has the idea of giving up one's own right or will.[5]

That's exactly what goes on in the 49er huddle. You have eleven strong-willed men with strong opinions. Yet in order for them to function as an effective unit, they choose to voluntarily give up their wills in order to follow the leadership of Montana.

Let me underscore the fact that this principle does not inhibit or restrain good communication. Even though Rice is subject to Montana, he is still free to give his opinion. Because Montana is a good leader, he values Rice's feedback. And the team as a whole submits to Montana's leadership because they have learned to trust him.

The same principle applies not only to football, but to the cockpit of a commercial jetliner. The tragic end of flight 1713 came about because the two men in the cockpit did not know how to work as a team. And isn't it interesting that one of the women questioned the leadership capabilities of the first officer based on his demeanor and appearance alone? There was something about him that caused her to wonder if he could be entrusted with such a significant responsibility. Tragically, her instincts were right. Dead right.

The same principle applies to marriage as well. The real version of Ephesians 5:22-23 goes like this:

> Wives, be subject to your own husbands, as to the Lord. For the husband is the head of the wife, as Christ also is the head of the church . . . (NASB).

One commentator makes a very appropriate statement:

> To the wife it should be said that the form your submission takes will vary according to the quality of your husband's leadership. If the husband is a godly man who has a biblical vision for the family and leads out in the things of the Spirit, a godly wife will rejoice in this leadership and support him in it. You will be no more squelched by this leadership than the disciples were squelched by the leadership of Jesus.[6]

Did you catch that first sentence and the emphasis upon the quality of the husband's leadership? It all goes back to trust. Trust is what motivates people to follow our leadership, whether at work or home. And trust must be earned, gentlemen.

John Gardner tells the following story: "I recall the senior partner of a law firm stressing to younger men and women in his firm the importance of client trust. One ambitious young lawyer asked how one went about winning trust, and the senior partner said dryly, 'Try being trustworthy.' "[7]

Authority is not a bad idea. Without it, society would spin off into anarchy. Edmund Burke once said, "An event has happened, upon which it is difficult to speak, and impossible to be silent." Burke was referring to the impeachment of Warren Hastings, the governor-general of India, in 1789.

In our day, the impeachment applies to male leadership in the home. I agree with Burke. This impeachment is difficult to talk about, but it's impossible to be silent. Especially since the idea of the husband being head of the wife has come under such attack *within* the church.

Some scholars have gone to great lengths to insist that the word *head* doesn't carry with it ideas of authority. According to them, "head" means "source." I won't go into all of the textual arguments on why there is a difference of opinion on the meaning of "head." [See the appendix for a more details on this issue.] But the significance of the discussion is this. If "head" doesn't mean authority, then God has not given to men the spiritual responsibility of leading their homes. Up until twenty years ago, that idea had never been seriously entertained in two thousand years of Christian scholarship.

The husband has been given authority in the home by God, just as the quarterback has it in the huddle and the captain has it in the cockpit. Male authority in the home is not a popular idea anymore. Maybe that's why the American family is in such trouble.

Scripture indicates that God holds the man responsible for decisions made in the family, just as the quarterback is responsible for decisions on the field and the airline captain is responsible for decisions in the cockpit.

One clear example is found in Genesis 3:1-13 when Adam and Eve were in the Garden. The account plainly shows that it was Eve who first succumbed to temptation and brought sin into the world. Adam, unfortunately, soon repeated the disobedient act. Yet when God approached them to discuss the matter, *He purposely sought out Adam first.* It would have made more sense for Him to have approached Eve first, unless of course, by the man's headship position, he was ultimately accountable for those choices, just as an executive vice-president of marketing is ultimately responsible for the decisions made in his department.

Richard Wirthlin, who was President Ronald Reagan's pollster, tells about the time he had to let his boss know his approval rating had fallen to a record low. The bad news came just one year after the assassination attempt, when Reagan's popularity was at a record high.

Normally, Wirthlin didn't go in to see the president alone. This time, no one would go with him. Reagan took one look at the lone Wirthlin and said, "Tell me the bad news." Wirthlin told him. Not only had his approval rating dived since the assassination attempt—it was the lowest approval rating of any president in his second year of office in the history of polls.

"Dick, don't worry," Reagan told him. "I'll just go out there and try to get assassinated again."[8]

Perhaps my popularity rating with some of you has nose-dived right here with this perspective on male headship in the home. Many think the idea of male headship went out with hula hoops, bell-bottoms, and eight-track cartridges. But before you assassinate my position, hear me out. I've found that what many people react to on this issue is not authority, but the wrong use of authority. What they're reacting to is *authoritarianism.*

Authoritarianism is something we *should* react to, whether it occurs in a oppressed country or a Christian home.

The Symptoms of Authoritarianism

A man has moved from proper authority to authoritarianism in his home when he demonstrates the following symptoms:

- he lacks interest in his wife's input and disregards her feelings,

- he forbids the children to discuss his decisions with him and is reluctant to let them make decisions on their own as they mature,

- he trusts few people,

- he displays an intense need to control those closest to him.

Authoritarianism is not ordained by God. But authority is. Authoritarianism doesn't work in Eastern Europe, or on winning football teams, or in effective homes.

In contrast to the "high control" authoritarian, the

mature man who practices biblical headship in the marriage relationship can be recognized by three characteristics:

- he loves his wife sacrificially,
- he loves his wife with understanding,
- he loves his wife with verbal praise.

A Mature Man Loves His Wife Sacrificially

Another look at Ephesians 5, verse 25 underscores that a husband's love is demonstrated by his willingness to sacrifice for his wife: "Husbands, love your wives, just as Christ also loved the church and gave himself up for her . . ."

Robert Wadlow (1918-1940) was the tallest man ever to challenge a tape measure. He was 8 feet, 11 inches. Calvin Phillips, who died in 1812, could stretch himself out to a full 2 feet, 2 inches. They were literally the long and short of it. Most of us are not that extreme in our dimensions. In fact, the average man in America is 5 feet 9 inches tall, weighs 162 pounds, and has a 31-inch waist.[9]

It's easy to measure physical size. Measuring sacrificial love is another story. We can measure the sacrificial love of Christ by looking to the cross. That has been the ultimate measurement of sacrifice for two thousand years.

But how does a wife measure the sacrificial love of her husband? For some reason, wives have the uncanny ability to measure our sacrificial love with the accuracy of a yardstick. They can recognize it from miles away. They intuitively know there is a direct correlation between service and sacrifice. And it usually comes out in the little things that spring from a right attitude.

Years ago in a humble hotel in Philadelphia, an elderly couple approached the night clerk and begged him for a room. It seems a convention was in town, and all hotels were booked full for the night.

"Are there any rooms left anywhere?" the old man inquired.

The clerk thought for a moment and realized his room was available since he was working the desk all night long. He gave his room to the elderly couple. At breakfast the next morning, the old couple invited the desk clerk to join them.

"Young man," said the elderly gentlemen, "you're too good a hotel man for this place. How would you like for me to build a big hotel for you in New York City?"

The elderly man was John Jacob Astor, who went on to build the famed Waldorf-Astoria hotel. And because of his service that came out of a willingness to sacrifice, that obscure and isolated night clerk eventually became one of the greatest hotel men in the world.[10]

Your wife may not be able to reward your sacrifice in the same way Astor could. But I guarantee you she will be just as impressed and appreciative.

A Mature Man Loves His Wife with Understanding

Most of us can identify with Peter. He was always putting his foot in his mouth or getting into some kind of difficulty. Peter was married. I'm sure that in the early years, like many of us, he was no prize to live with. He probably had much to learn about being a good husband. Toward the end of his life, as he had mellowed and matured, he wrote these words: "You husbands likewise, live with your wives in an understanding way . . ." (1 Peter 3:7, NASB).

The word *understanding* carries with it the idea of insight and tactfulness.[11] No one enjoys being misunderstood. It's one of the truly miserable experiences in life. The woman who has a husband who knows when to put his arms around her and simply hold her close will inevitably feel understood. Sometimes that's the most insightful and tactful thing we can do. Don't offer a solution, just hold her. I don't think that came easy to Peter; it certainly doesn't come naturally to me. But I'm learning.

Mrs. Winston Churchill was sitting next to General Charles DeGaulle at a luncheon, and during one of the many silences found herself thinking how difficult Mrs. DeGaulle's life must be. Her thoughts were interrupted by General DeGaulle saying to her, "It must be very difficult, madame, being the wife of Mr. Churchill."[12]

What is difficult for any wife, regardless of whom she is married to, is to be misunderstood. Peter knew that a woman who felt understood would have little difficulty in following the leadership of a husband who led her is such an understanding way.

A Mature Man Loves His Wife with Verbal Praise

Peter give us another piece of strategic advice in verse 7 when he writes, ". . . and grant her honor as a fellow heir of the grace of life, so that your prayers may not be hindered."

The word translated "honor" carries with it the

idea of value. A mature man provides the kind of leadership to his wife that lets her know how valuable she is to him.

Verbal praise is a rare commodity in our world. That's why Mark Twain said he could live for sixty days off one compliment. You may deeply appreciate your wife in your heart, but when was the last time you verbally expressed your appreciation to her? Perhaps you don't remember, but I would be willing to bet that *she* does. It's easy to forget the importance of verbal praise in the routine of day-to-day to living. But as O. A. Battista has observed, "An error doesn't become a mistake until you refuse to correct it."

There are severe consequence for the man who refuses to correct his errors with his wife. Peter puts it on the table. If you do not live with your wife in an understanding way, and let her know she is valuable to you, your prayers will be hindered. That's how serious this matter is. You may be the most articulate man of prayer in your church, but if you are not implementing this scriptural prescription, you're wasting your breath. God will not respond.

The man who is careful not to miss his time of prayer, yet neglects his wife's emotional needs, fits the description that Daniel O'Connor gave of the British attorney, Lord Manners:

That's the most sensible looking man talking nonsense I ever saw.

Mature leadership from a husband makes it easy for a wife to coexist in the marriage cockpit with him. A man who treats his wife with care and respect will do more than just coexist with her. They will both actually enjoy the ride.

If I could define headship in a nutshell, I would put it this way: Biblical headship for a husband is giving the best of all that he is to those under his care and authority.

I would define submission in a complimentary manner: Biblical submission for a wife is giving the best of all that she is to the one that is in authority over her.[13]

Several hundred years ago, Martin Luther described it this way: "Let the wife make the husband glad to come home, and let him make her sorry to see him leave." That's good teamwork in anybody's book.

There is more to good teamwork than just the Montana-Rice principle. The mature husband, like the experienced captain in the cockpit, has discovered the wisdom and the protection that is brought to his leadership by the safeguard of mutual accountability.

Mutual Accountability

Gerhard Frost once said that the reason mountain climbers are tied together is to keep the sane ones from going home. That's what marriage is. It is two people tied together as they climb the mountain of life. They have to work as a team. They cannot work independently of each other. In order to reach the summit, they must be interdependent. It takes teamwork to climb a mountain, to fly a 747, and to keep a marriage fresh and alive. It also takes mutual accountability.

Sometimes when a couple gets married, we'll say that they have "tied the knot." So they have . . . just like the mountain climbers who tie the knot to keep tabs on one another in case of a sudden blizzard or accident. Accountability is a protection for both parties.

Let me give you a simple definition of accountability that I heard from Chuck Swindoll years ago: *Accountability is a willingness to explain your actions.* Mutual accountability simply means that husband and wife are to be accountable to one another. You explain your actions to her, and she explains hers to you. If mutual accountability had been practiced on flight 1713, it never would have gone down. Mutual accountability insures that a plane crash will not occur due to a mistake in the cockpit.

The vast majority of men have wives who want their husbands to win. She is on your team. When a man begins to understand that, he views his wife in a new way. Gentlemen, your wife is a strategic gift to you! She has eyes that see what you don't, a mind that assimilates information from a different perspective, a heart with sensitivities you do not possess, and a personality with strengths that offset your weaknesses. That's a built-in protection for you. That's why you must tap into her perspective as you lead your family. When she offers a constructive criticism, learn to listen to her with an open mind. It may save you from accumulating ice on your wings.

Ted Engstom makes a poignant observation when he writes:

> I've noticed that behavior put under close scrutiny tends to change *for the better.* People who are made accountable to a mentor, to a group of friends . . . become more serious about changing their behavior . . . When there is improvement, invariably it means that a person has been called to account. An unaccountable spouse is living

on the edge of risk; an unaccountable CEO is in danger of taking his company down a wrong road; an unaccountable pastor has too much authority; an unaccountable counselor has too much responsibility and needs too much wisdom to be able to handle it on his own.

Between a husband and a wife there is a built-in accountability. If there is a breakdown in accountability, a breakdown in the marriage is imminent.[14]

Let's say a husband decides he wants to buy a wide-screen TV. The mature husband realizes that such an item comes under the heading of a major purchase. He's looking at two thousand bucks minimum. Because it is a high-cost item, the mature husband will sit down with his wife, explain why he wants to get it, where the money is going to come from in the budget, and how the larger picture will keep him from going blind at an early age.

The mature husband realizes his wife's perspective on the purchase is important. She may remind him that they recently discussed putting a new deck and patio in the backyard. There isn't money to do both, and she thinks the new addition to the backyard is more important. As they discuss the issue, they will probably come to a decision both feel good about. And not only has a good decision been made, but they both know and understand the reasons behind the decision.

Contrast that process with the following scenario. On Saturday morning, the wife goes one direction to run errands, and the husband goes another to accomplish his list. When she gets home, he's sitting there watching the NCAA Final Four on his brand new, $2,500 Mitsubishi wide-screen TV. To him, it's no big deal. Sometimes he buys new socks, sometimes he buys a new TV. As General Carl Spaatz said about one of his fellow officers, "He thinks things through very carefully before he goes off half-cocked."

Now if this guy is head of his home, can he go out and make that kind of financial decision? Yes. Is that the wise way to make such a major purchase? No. The mature man makes himself mutually accountable to his wife by including her in the decision-making process. The immature man goes off and does what he wants without considering his wife's perspective. He has no intention of explaining his actions.

That is poor leadership, no matter how you cut it. Eventually such a man is going to make a major mistake, because he isn't willing to explain his actions and process the feedback from his wife.

The Intimidation Factor

One way that some men keep from being mutually accountable is through intimidation. Almost thirty years ago, when Nikita Khrushchev visited America, he gave a press conference at the Washington Press Club. The first question from the floor—handled through an interpreter—was: "Today you talked about the hideous rule of your predecessor, Stalin. You were one of his closest aides and colleagues during those years. What were you doing all that time?"

Khrushchev's face got red. *"Who asked that?"* he roared.

All five hundred faces turned down.

"Who asked that?" he insisted. Nothing. "That's what I was doing," he said.[15]

Neither Khrushchev nor the reporters spoke up because of intimidation. And intimidation can also be present in the cockpit. It was described to me in a recent conversation with a man who has been in commercial aviation for over thirty years.

The scenario goes something like this. The captain and co-captain have gone through their respective checklists before take-off. The plane is cleared for take-off and sits ready to go. Suddenly the co-captain becomes aware of a dangerous buildup of ice on the wings. Should he speak up? By all definitions, that is his job.

Unfortunately, in some cases, the captain is so "high control" with his authority, that the co-captain becomes intimidated. Some captains are so protective of their superior position that they do not allow the co-captain to do anything during the entire flight. In essence, the co-captain might as well not even be present.

In this particular high control scenario, the captain may take the suggestion of the co-captain as a bad reflection on his authority and expertise. Not only that, but the two of them must fly together in that cockpit for a full month. If they start out on a wrong footing, the captain could make his co-captain's life miserable. Thus, the copilot could become hesitant to speak up when the situation demands it.

Let me hasten to assure you that not all captain/co-captain relationships are like the one I've described. But according to my friend, it has become a big enough problem that the airline industry is taking steps to keep "intimidation" from becoming a hindrance to teamwork in the cockpit. The risks are just too high when a captain is not open to a second opinion.

What are the consequences when a qualified first officer remains silent when he should speak up? The lives of every person on board, including his own, are endangered! His role is that of a team player, and he had better not let "intimidation" keep him from doing his job.

This very problem can occur in the marriage 747. A "high control" husband can easily develop the same attitude that some captains have adopted. He is going to run his home the way he wants, and he doesn't want suggestions from anyone—especially his wife. After all, he may think, according to the Scripture, it's her "job" to submit to his authority.

This is one reason that Christian marriages are going down in flames all over America. If a husband has a distorted view of what the Scripture means by "submission," he can intimidate his wife to the point that she will be afraid to speak up even when his leadership is clearly off-base. He's getting ready to fly straight into the side of a mountain, but she's too afraid of how he'll react if she says something.

Some guys think that a wife's submission means that she lets him do anything he wants. Nothing could be further from the truth. It's just as wrong for a wife to remain quiet as it would be for a first officer who sees ice on the wings. Now let's face it, most first officers will speak up when lives are on the line. But it's possible for a first officer or a wife to become so intimidated by a dominant personality that their fear of speaking up would actually overshadow their fear of an accident.

When General William J. (Wild Bill) Donovan appeared before the Joint Chiefs of Staff in 1942, one of the chiefs asked him to explain the term "psychological warfare." Donovan is said to have responded, "It's what you fellows practice on each other."[16] Intimidation is just another form of psychological warfare, and it has no place in the home of a man who is following Jesus Christ.

The Straight Scoop on Submission

We need to get one thing straight. Submission is not just an issue for wives. Yes, Ephesians 5:22 does say, "Wives, be subject to your own husbands" (NASB). But submission is a responsibility that applies to every one of us. Submission is inescapable and universal. Everyone submits.

A young sentry, on guard duty for the first time, had orders not to admit any car unless it had a special identification seal. The first unmarked car the sentry stopped contained a general. When the general told his driver to go right on through, the sentry politely said, "I'm new at this, sir. Who do I shoot first, you or the driver?"

The sentry had it right. Everybody submits. Submission is for generals, presidents, teachers, students, accountants, attorneys, Central American dictators, and wives. It's also for husbands. No one escapes submission. We are all under authority.

Scripture gives several examples:

• Spiritual leaders have authority over a church congregation (Hebrews 13:17).

- Governing authorities (elected officials, police officers, etc.) have authority over citizens (Romans 13:1).

- Husbands have authority in the home (Ephesians 5:22).

- Parents have authority over their children (Ephesians 6:1).

- Children have authority over their pets (No kidding!) (Genesis 1:28).

Let's face it. None of us like the idea of submitting to someone else. The classic American phrase is "No one's going to tell ME what to do!"

I believe Scripture teaches that the husband is the head of the marriage relationship, and the wife is to ultimately submit to his authority. But I also believe that a man should not demand submission from his wife. Instead, he should be such an exemplary model of submission to the authorities in his own life, that he provides the kind of leadership at home that is easy to follow.

Mutual Submission

Mutual submission simply means that you each consider the other person over yourself. There is a good reason that Paul begins this whole passage on husband/wife relationships with the command to "submit to one another out of reverence for Christ" (Ephesians 5:21). Many a man has camped on verses 22-24 without ever noticing the context. Submission is not just as issue for wives . . . it is a Christian issue that affects every member of the body of Christ.

For me, the best example of mutual submission is

to watch a great basketball team like the Lakers or Celtics. The best teams are made up of players who practice this principle. When Kevin McHale sets a screen so that Larry Bird can get open to take a pass from Dennis Johnson, that is mutual submission at work. There are five guys playing, but only one guy can take the shot. So McHale submits by setting a screen, Johnson submits by passing instead of shooting, and Bird submits by following his missed shot, getting the rebound, and dishing it off to Robert Parrish . . . who jams it in for two.

If you follow the Celtics over an entire season, you'll notice that in one game Bird will be the high scorer, another night Parrish, then McHale, then Bird, then Johnson, and so on. In other words, in any given game they go with the guy who has the hot hand. That's mutual submission. Each player wants to win and is willing to "place himself under" in order to get the victory.

Let me be clear. Mutual submission does not mean that the husband and wife take turns being the head of the home. That is the man's permanent assignment. It does mean that the husband demonstrates and models the concept of submission in his own life when the situation calls for such a response. Mutual submission is just another way of describing servant leadership for the husband and loving submission for the wife. *It is at the core of both biblical headship and biblical submission.*

It means, gentlemen, that you take the lead in your submission to Christ to such an extent that you become a model for your wife. A man's willingness to serve his wife and meet her needs will provide an environment and a stimulus for her to respond in submission to his leadership. If she sees that kind of attitude in you, and senses that you are diligently seeking to follow hard after Christ, it will be much easier for her to relax in your leadership in the home. I have yet to meet a Christian woman whose husband provides this kind of leadership who has difficulty with the idea of biblical submission. When a husband loves his wife as the Scripture commands, it's a win-win situation for everyone.

In other words, the captain can remove the atmosphere of "intimidation," and replace it with openness, encouragement, and appreciation. Sam Goldwyn, the president of MGM studios, once said to his staff, "I want you to tell me exactly what's wrong with me and MGM. Even if it costs you your job."

That is not mutual submission. It is one-sided intimidation that God never intended to be the pattern for male leadership.

"Just As"

We've said quite a bit about the principles that make for good teamwork in marriage. Maybe I've said too much. If this seems like a lot to absorb, let me bottom-line it for you. When it comes right down to it, there are only two words a man has to remember about leading his wife . . . "just as."

If you can't recall anything else in this chapter, just remember those two words and you'll have it all. In Ephesians 5: 25, Paul writes: "Husbands, love your wives, *just as* Christ also loved the church and gave himself up for her."

In other words, if you are not sure how to lead or how to respond in a given situation, take your cue from Christ and do it just as He loved the church. Christ is our role model for loving our wives.

Steve DeVore has built a multi-million dollar company on the principle of role modeling. DeVore is president of SyberVision, a company that markets instructional video and audio tapes on everything from golf to skiing to weight control. This is not some kind of mystical New Age approach to learning, but rather the master-apprentice relationship put to work in different settings.

When DeVore was in college, he happened to watch a bowling tournament on television. As he paid close attention to the movements of the bowlers, the thought struck him that if he could emulate their movements, he could probably achieve the same results.

After watching the bowlers closely for thirty minutes, he got in his car and drove to the local bowling alley. He got an alley, picked out a ball, and for the next thirty minutes he did *just as* the professional bowlers had done on TV. He threw nine straight strikes and recorded a score of 278. His highest score up to that point was 163. By emulating a proficient role model, he improved his performance by 115 pins. But the key was *just as*. He had to do it *just as* the pros.

Gentlemen, if we will pay close attention to the methods of Jesus Christ, we can fly our marriage 747s with more harmony and satisfaction in the cockpit than we ever thought possible.

If you need more guidance, check in with your Lord in the control tower. His calm voice can guide you and your co-captain through the darkest of nights to a perfect landing . . . together.

The Birth of
a Tangent

*Tangent: To break off suddenly from a line
of action or train of thought and pursue
another course.*

Webster

The professor could see he was losing his students. Eyes were wandering, pens doodling. He
needed to get his charges back, and quick. So he
called in Frank Zappa.

"We've been talking about journalism in general,"
the prof intoned, "but does anybody here know what
'rock journalism' in particular is?"

Silence. Most eyes stopped wandering. Most pens
quit doodling. Many quizzical expressions seemed to
ask, *What did he just say?*

"Here's Frank Zappa's definition," the prof continued: "'Rock journalism is people who can't write, interviewing people who can't talk, for people who can't read.' Do you think he's right?"

The class howled. The prof just smiled. His little tangent had worked. He had his class back; now he could continue.

Although the prof's little impromptu question broke with his main train of thought, it was the very thing that kept his class moving ahead. Tangents are sometimes useful for that. We need them to keep moving ahead. At least, I'm hoping that's true, because a tangent's just what we're about to go off on.

I've been assuming that if you have read this far, you are a Christian male who is either married or one day hopes to be married. I've also assumed that if you are married, you either have children or hope to have children. I have additionally assumed that you single guys who hope one day to marry also desire to have children. In short, I've assumed that, regardless of your present marital status, you would like one day to have children.

And that is precisely where I may have made a big error.

An incredibly strong trend is sweeping America and picking up steam with every passing day. It is the trend toward childless marriages. And this is where I want to go off on my tangent.

I know that some of you reading this endorse that viewpoint. Quite frankly, I want to challenge your thinking on this issue. As a matter of fact, my goal is to persuade you to change your mind. To be even more specific, my short-term goal for you married guys is that you would be so convinced I'm right, that in the next nine to twelve months you'll need to paint the extra bedroom either pink or blue. How's that for putting my cards on the table?

Before I really get into this tangent, I need to say a couple of things. First of all, this tangent will be under semi-control. As best as I can tell at this point, it is going to be a tangent of approximately six to seven pages. That's a long tangent but a short chapter.

Second, I should point out that if I don't go out on this tangent, the next chapter could become a waste of time. If we Christians who are capable of having children don't have them, then you tell me where the masculine men and feminine women for the next generation are going to come from. And if there are no masculine men and feminine women for the next generation or the ones to follow, then you might as well go ahead and shut this country down.

The Two Kinds of Childless Christian Couples

Over the years, I've met scores of couples with broken hearts. The reason is simple. They've tried doctor after doctor, read book after book, endured test after test, but they have not been able to conceive. The thought of not having a child breaks their hearts. Many of them, after years of trying, would readily adopt a child. But with the abortion rate in this country somewhere near two million a year, there just aren't many children available.

It's abhorrent that the most dangerous place for a child in America is in the womb. Especially when those children could be taken in by couples who would love and care for them. These couples with grieving hearts realize the wisdom found in Psalm 127:3 (NASB):

> Behold, children are a gift of the LORD;
> The fruit of the womb is a reward.

These couples would do anything to have a child. One such friend called me a few years ago to explain that he and his wife were willing to leave a tremendous situation on the East Coast and move to the West Coast, even though it would mean a drastic cut in their income. Why would they do that? Just one reason: There was a baby available for adoption. Because of some conflicting laws in two different states, they would have to pick up and move to another state to get the child. They were willing to do it, but unfortunately the details couldn't be worked out.

What would drive this couple to do something so drastic? They are not impulsive people; they are quite mature. They were willing to go to such lengths, however, because they knew that children are a gift from the Lord. I am pleased to report that several years later their broken hearts were healed (and I think you can guess why).

I have also met a second group of Christian couples. They are different from the first group in that they have *chosen* not to have children. They have the ability to conceive, they just don't want to. My question to those of you who have made such a choice is this: Why? When all is said and done, what is the real reason you have chosen not to bring new life into your home?

There may be excellent reasons why you have chosen not to have children. But this decision has such long-range consequences that it needs to be carefully analyzed in light of Scripture.

Please note that I am not referring to family planning. In my judgment, it is good stewardship to think through how many children we are going to have and when they might come along. If God has another plan in mind, He has His ways of stepping in and altering your plan. I can personally vouch for that! As always, His plan was superior to ours. We're very, very glad He set aside our plans.

The issue here is not when to have a family, but choosing not to have one. I have heard several reasons offered for such a choice, but I honestly don't think they hold up under close scrutiny. A couple of currently popular objections:

• *This is not the kind of world that I want to bring a child into.*

My response is simply, why not? How do you know that God won't use your child to make a significant contribution to changing the world? If the mother of Jonas Salk had felt that way, there would still be hundreds of thousands of kids crippled by polio. If Billy Graham's parents were of that persuasion, there would be several million people whose lives would not have been touched by the gospel. If Abraham Lincoln's parents had made that choice, this country might never have survived the internal hemorrhaging of civil war.

"But not every child is a Salk, a Graham, or a Lincoln," you say. You are right. In fact, it was Lincoln who said, "God must love common men. He made so many of them." Let's face it. That's what most of us are. We're just average people. Do you remember the book, *I'm O.K., You're O.K.?* I once heard Moishe Rosen, founder of Jews for Jesus, suggest that someone write a book titled, *I'm So-So, You're So-So.* Moishe is right. Most of us are just so-so.

There's nothing wrong, however, with being average or so-so. Behind every Salk, Graham, and Lincoln, there are hundreds of average and so-so people who have influenced their lives. Every child brought into this world can make a significant contribution. *Christian homes are the salt of the earth. But if we stop producing salt, what will happen to our influence?*

Perhaps more than ever before, the desperate needs of our culture demand godly homes which produce godly children. God will protect and care for your children. Ultimately, they belong to Him anyway. We should not let the erosion of our culture prevent us from having children and trusting God to use them to make a difference. Go ahead and have kids and give your concerns to the Lord. I like what Mary C. Crowley said: "Every night I give my worries over to the Lord. He's going to be up all night anyway."

A second popular objection to having children:

* *We can't afford to have children right now.*

I want to let you in on a secret. You can *never* afford to have kids. It is never financially convenient for your wife to get pregnant. You could have a net worth of thirty-five million bucks and still not find it financially convenient to have kids. If you wait until you're financially secure to have children, you'll never have them.

If you really stop and think about it, financial security is a figment of the American mind. It could all be gone tomorrow. The only security in the entire world is found in Jesus Christ. Every other kind of security is an illusion.

I'm all for financial planning. But if you let financial planning get in the way of having kids, you are making a major error. You're going to miss out on the joy that money can never buy.

Let me bottom-line my response to this objection. When people say they can't afford kids, too many times I think what they are really saying is, "If we have kids, we will have to lower our standard of living." If that is your real reason, you are making a decision not based on scriptural wisdom but on contemporary propaganda. You may indeed have to lower your standard of living—in fact, you probably will—but I guarantee that your quality of life will go up dramatically.

Not too long ago, *Newsweek* ran a revealing article on the trend in America for couples to choose against having kids. They painted the scenario like this:

> He works long and often unpredictable hours at the office. So does she. No time to cook at the end of the day: they usually meet for dinner at a trendy restaurant or one of them stops to pick up gourmet takeout on the way home. Their car is an expensive, sporty two-seater—just right for the weekend getaways. Their white living room rug has never known the muddy footprints of little feet. These are not traditional scenes; there are no kids around. But more and more couples are painting a new kind of American family portrait—one with just two faces, the husband's and the wife's.[1]

In this fascinating article, a number of childless couples were interviewed. Listen to some of their reasons for choosing not to have children:

> "There's a real economic burden to raising children," says Nancy Baron . . . Baron and her husband, Neil Osterweil, also a writer, decided against children before they were married last year. "Sometimes," she says, "Neil and I joke that we'd like to adopt an 18-year-old, complete with college tuition."[2]

What's the bottom line here? Selfishness. Another couple says:

> "We could not lead the kind of life we have if we had kids." Janet Young, 38, a molecular biologist . . . and her husband, Harold Goldstein, 41, a professor of civil engineering, like to travel and rock climb. "This is a prime-time in our lives," says Goldstein. "If we had a kid, we wouldn't be as active." He adds: "I guess I'm selfish. I like to do things for myself. I'm just not ready to sacrifice my time to a kid."[3]

He's definitely right about one thing. He is selfish.

Reading through this article reminded me of what Soren Kierkegaard once said: "Most men pursue pleasure with such breathless haste that they hurry past it." It appears to me that's exactly what these people are doing. In their zeal to get every drop of pleasure out of life, they are neglecting the long-term benefits and satisfactions that come from having a family. These people have chosen immediate gratification over delayed satisfaction.

In my opinion, microwave popcorn is inferior to what you get out of a popper. Sure, you have to wait longer to get the popcorn, but it's worth the wait. It takes wisdom to wait for the best. Some people are so hungry for popcorn that they will settle for the inferior and miss the superior. That's what these childless couples are doing. They want their pleasure quickly out of the microwave. They don't realize the pleasure they have chosen is nothing but husks compared to the real thing.

As far as I can tell from the article, none of these people claim to be Christians. What concerns me is that more and more *Christian* couples are choosing not to have children for the same reasons. This trend of choosing not to have children is making serious inroads into the evangelical church. I've talked to too many Christian couples who offer the same reasoning. To be frank, it seems that some Christians couples would translate Psalm 127:3 like this:

> Behold, children are a curse from the Lord;
> The fruit of the womb is inconvenient.

My question to couples who have chosen not to have children revolves around this verse. What is the real reason behind your choice to remain childless? Is it selfishness? If it is, then you should reevaluate your decision. You may miss some of the greatest blessings God has in store for you. Deciding to have kids may mean you'll have to give up your BMW. But it's worth it.

Before I married, I used to have a BMW. I had a lot of fun with that car. I now have three kids and no BMW. I have an Audi that's eight years old with more than 100,000 miles on it. Hundreds of M & M's are crushed into the fibers of its carpet, and teenage mutant Ninja turtles lurk under the seats. When my daughter Rachel was three, she crawled up on the front bumper of my two-month-old car and sketched a picture on my hood with a rock. Her artwork is still there.

My BMW used to be flawless. With three kids, my Audi is anything but. Yet my life has greatly improved. God has brought more blessing into my life through these three children than any material possession ever could. Trust me. It's a lot more fun raising kids than BMWs.

It should be said that the idea of a couple choosing not to have children is foreign to Scripture. Even the *Newsweek* article pointed out the downside of this decision:

> Couples who wait too long and find they are unable to have children face a particular painful situation. It is still harder for a 38-year-old woman to get pregnant than it is for a 22-year-old woman. When Bobbi and Lynn Bender were married 20 years ago, they decided to postpone parenthood until they had established careers. They began trying to have kids when Bobbi was in her early 30s. Nothing happened. "For years I stayed on the Pill out of fear of getting pregnant," says Bobbi, now 40 and the associate director of finance at the University of Chicago Medical Center. "Then I find out I can't have children."[4]

She doesn't know if she would have been able to get pregnant earlier, but because she started so late, even adoption—the only alternative—is unlikely. Most agencies prefer to find homes for their infant charges with younger couples. In any case, Bender and her husband, Lynn, 43, the director of physical planning and construction at the university, feel they are too set in their ways to become new parents. Nonetheless, says Bobbi, "there are times when I wake up on Mothers's Day and burst into tears." When she meets couples who are able to have children, but don't, she is shocked. "I think they are going to regret that decision once they find that not being able to have a child has become a fact rather than a choice," she says. "You have this hollow core inside of you that will never be fulfilled."

J. B. Phillips once translated Romans 12:2 like this: "Don't let the world around you squeeze you into its own mould." If you are one of those couples who have decided not to have kids, whose mold are you being poured into? If the real reason is selfishness, admit it, then join the club. We're all selfish. Selfish to the core.

It's been my experience that those who are willing to give up the immediate gratification that comes from choosing a childless marriage quickly see a change taking place in their lives once a baby shows up. The change is this: God begins dealing with your own selfishness by giving you someone to care for who is infinitely more selfish than you. Babies are not only the cutest creatures on the face of the earth, they are by far the most selfish.

The way God deals with my own selfishness is to give me someone to serve who has zero interest in serving me. You can't tell me that God doesn't have a sense of humor. Not too many people in the world could out-selfish me one-on-one. But every time we've had a baby, I've met my match. Each of my kids resembled me. I don't mean they looked like me, I mean they were as selfish as me. That meant that *somebody* in the family was going to have to grow up. Guess who was nominated?

God begins to take away our selfishness by giving us children for whom we would do things we would never do for anyone else. You guys with kids know what I'm talking about. When you have a baby, you find yourself getting up every couple of hours to make sure he or she is okay. Your wife will get up every two to three hours to see if the baby is hungry. My wife loves me, but she never did that for me.

You'll find yourself in the bathroom at two in the morning with the shower going full blast. You, however, won't be in the shower. You'll be sitting on the toilet seat holding your little girl who has the croup, since the only thing that will break it up is plenty of hot steam. I doubt that's what you'd normally choose to do at that time of night. But you have as much love in your heart for your little girl as she has congestion in her lungs. So you sit there and love her and try to remember what it was like to sleep eight hours straight.

If God blesses you with children, you'll be taking part in one of the most significant accomplishments a man can enjoy.

Some guys head their own corporations by age thirty-five. Big deal.

Some guys win five gold medals at the Olympics. Big deal.

Some guys climb Mount Everest. Big deal.

Some guys swim the length of the Pacific under water without taking a breath. Big deal.

In my book, none of those exploits come close to the man who has learned to change a dirty diaper without throwing up. That's what I call a big deal. Especially when you can do it without an oxygen mask. It's also what Jesus called being a servant.

There are hundreds of little and big things you will do for your kids that you wouldn't do for anyone else. Those afflicted with great selfishness, like myself, will find that as the years go by, God will use your children to chip away at the selfishness clogging your life. Before long, you'll find yourself doing things for other people you never thought possible. That's what the Bible refers to as spiritual growth.

Psalm 127:3 is right. Children are a gift from the Lord.

May He reward you with them!

My wife and I have been blessed by three little lives that have given us more joy than all of the travel, gourmet food, BMWs, and designer clothes that the Gold Card can buy. May God bless you with as much joy! And may you be smart enough to recognize a good deal when you see it. And, by the way . . . as long as you're going to have one, you might as well go for two, three, or four. I know you can't afford it. But you'll sure have a great time. You'll also be very tired. But that's all right. You can rest in heaven.

End of tangent.

CHAPTER NINE

How to Raise Masculine Sons and Feminine Daughters

Men are generally more careful of the breed of their horses and dogs than of their children.
William Penn

If you could see me in this office right now, it would crack you up. By conservative estimate, I've got somewhere around forty books spread out on my desk, the floor, and reaching into the closet. Scattered around are numerous articles from various psychological journals, sociological monographs, quotes from Margaret Mead, Gloria Steinem, George Gilder, William Buckley, James Dobson and Mr. T. I'm loaded for bear on this topic—and that's just my problem. I've got too much information.

I'd been wrestling with this problem for days when I finally decided to give it a rest. I went down to the mall to finish my Christmas shopping. All I had left was to buy my wife some clothes. I went down to the women's department at Dillard's and acted like I knew what I was doing . . . and then it happened.

Somewhere between Liz Claiborne and Evan-Picone, it hit me. Everything I wanted to say about raising masculine sons and feminine daughters was addressed in one verse of the New Testament. Every piece of research I have regarding the development of a child's sexual identity is either directly or indirectly related to this one verse. Every book, every article, every quote, and every statistic merely reflects from different perspectives the principles contained in Ephesians 6:4:

> And, fathers, do not provoke your children
> to anger; but bring them up in the discipline
> and instruction of the Lord (NASB).

Ephesians 6:4 is a compass that enables a father to give his children correct guidance toward finding their sexual identities.

A compass is invaluable in the wilderness because it gives accurate direction. If someone is confused and unsure about north, south, east or west, a compass will give correct information. According to Webster, a compass is "a device of determining directions by means of a magnetic needle . . . turning freely on a pivot and pointing to the magnetic north." A compass helps us get out of confusing circumstances and move toward our desired destination.

That describes exactly the role of a father. We live in a world of confusing and wrong sexual information.

An Ephesians 6:4 father is the compass boys read in order to find the correct path to masculinity and girls read to find the right road to femininity.

Scripture outlines four reference points for fathers that enable them to point their children to an accurate, God-given, sexual identity. Just as a compass has four key marks—north, south, east, and west—so a Christian father is given four directions for pointing his children toward their correct sexual identity. Whether he knows it or not, his children are reading him like a compass every day of their lives.

This is no oversimplification. If men would implement this verse in their lives, the issue of their children's sexual identity would take care of itself. If a man would consistently apply this passage, his boys would be masculine and his girls would be feminine.

This wasn't much of an issue when we were growing up because the basic role models were in place. Homosexuals or bisexuals had little influence or visibility in our culture. But with influences like MTV (I think that stands for Mutant Television), our kids see celebrities who deliberately attempt to distort the differences between male and female.

Why is this sexual identity thing such a big deal? I'll let John Piper step up to the microphone to answer that: "The tendency today is to stress the equality of men and women by minimizing the unique significance of maleness and femaleness. It is taking a tremendous toll on generations of young men and women who do not know what it means to be a man or a woman. Confusion over the meaning of sexual personhood is epidemic . . . The consequence . . . is more divorce, more homosexuality, more sexual abuse, more promiscuity, more social awkwardness, and more emotional distress and suicide that comes with the loss of God-given identity."[1]

That's why it's such a big deal.

A man once asked to meet with me privately after I presented a talk on male leadership in the home. He told me that he and his wife had been Christians for thirty years and had reared five boys in a Christian home. Two of the five had become practicing homosexuals. This man had a broken heart. There wasn't much I could say to him. The compass had malfunctioned sometime in the early years of his boys' development. Something went wrong somewhere, and two of his boys now have distorted views of who they are as men.

Let me shoot straight with you. If we will function as the loving heads of our homes, respect and love our wives, and follow the guidelines of Ephesians 6:4, our children will not grow up to be homosexuals. I pastored for ten years in the San Francisco Bay area and counseled with more than a few homosexuals. Without exception, every one of them came from a home where the basic principles of Ephesians 5:22-6:4 were not implemented.

Homosexuals are not born, they are made.

In a book highly endorsed by the National Institutes of Health, *Growing Up Straight*, Peter Wyden reveals that:

> Research findings overwhelmingly indicate that homosexuals are not born but bred . . . there is increasing agreement that homosexuals rarely (if ever) occur without some important (or controlling) contribution from parents.

Many parents underestimate their own importance as models for the behavior of their children especially while the children are still young . . . they should appreciate that a mother's acceptance of her role as a truly feminine woman will communicate itself to a daughter at a remarkably early age; and that a mother's respect for the father's role as head of the family will help a small boy grow up to be masculine. On the other hand, if parents themselves are unsure about what constitutes appropriate male and female behavior today—or, especially if they are competitive with each other—their children are bound to become confused about their own place in the scheme of things.[2]

You would be surprised at how many homosexuals in San Francisco can quote verse after verse from the Bible. It's shocking to realize how many of them were raised in Christian homes and evangelical churches. In every case I have seen where they were so raised, their fathers were either spiritually anorexic or bulimic. These children may have had the Scripture drilled into them at home and church, but somewhere along the line, their fathers did not give them the accurate bearings they so desperately needed. They were reading a compass that confused them about who they were and how they were to view themselves.

Either the father was passive and the mother was dominant, or the father was so hard and brutal that the boy was driven away to identify solely with the tenderness and warmth of his mother. Somewhere the compass malfunctioned.

Children without strong role models in the home

are going to become hopelessly confused by today's conflicting cultural messages. Weldon Hardenbrook cites an article in *People* magazine: "A psychologist recently asked his 7-year-old nephew, 'Is Michael Jackson a boy or girl?' The boy thought for a moment before replying, 'Both.' "[3]

I agree with George Gilder: "I do not want my son to be told that he does not have to be masculine to succeed as a man—that he can be happily supported by a mothering wife and never really grow up. I do not want to see my daughters grow up to be like the feminist leaders now reportedly longing to have children as they approach their fifties. I do not want my wife to feel she is unequal to me if she earns less money than I do, or unequal to the careerist women I meet in my work. I understand that sexual liberalism chiefly liberates men from their families, and I love my family more than I long to relive a bachelor freedom or marry a coed. I understand the terrible losses inflicted by sexual liberalism on the men and women I know who try to live by its remorseless egalitarian code, who attempt to twist their lives and bodies into the unisex mold, who tangle in loveless sterility on the procrustean beds of emancipation."[4]

None of us want that for our children. Yet what most men don't realize is how central they are to the development of their children's sexual identity. If you don't think your kids read you like a compass, then listen to the startling comment that Sueann Robinson Ambrom makes in her book, *Child Development*:

> In gender role development, the evidence points to fathers as having the more important influence, not only in fostering a male

self-concept in boys, but femininity in girls. Mothers do contribute to their daughters' adoption of the feminine role, but have little influence on the masculinity of their sons.[5]

Our role as fathers is more critical now than at any time in history. Just this afternoon, I received a newsletter from The Family Research Council in Washington, D.C., one of the finest and most strategic Christian organizations in the world. It represents pro-family concerns in the halls of Congress as new legislation is considered and debated.

Gary Bauer, president of the council, writes these startling words: "The homosexual rights movement becomes more aggressive each day. This movement wants more than 'tolerance.' Its final goal is for homosexuality to be considered acceptable and normal. These folks will not stop until they have been granted all the rights and benefits of traditional married couples. Here, too, our children are at risk. *A nationwide campaign is now under way, already endorsed by the National Education Association and the American Civil Liberties Union, to place gay and lesbian counselors in every public school in America to help children decide and deal with their 'sexual identity'.* Such a program is already being implemented in some Los Angeles schools."[6]

We are living in days of exceptional evil. Our schools are handing out compasses deliberately designed to counter the truth of God. We have been given exceptional responsibilities as fathers in a culture that is going morally berserk. We must do our work of compassing well, for the survival and stability of our children is at stake.

Most men I know are concerned about this issue of masculinity and femininity. They are concerned that their boys turn out to be masculine and their girls feminine. Let's jump into Ephesians 6:4 and pull out the reference points that will enable us to give our children the direction they need to embrace their God-appointed sexual identities.

Moral Landmark #1:
Fathers Should Raise Their Children in Fairness

If a man is fair with his kids, he will not provoke them to anger. A passage in Colossians parallel to Ephesians 6:4 says:

Fathers, do not exasperate your children,
that they may not lose heart (3:21, NASB).

The idea behind the word *exasperate* is "do not embitter." This complements perfectly the word used in Ephesians 6:4 translated "provoke them to anger." The meaning here is "to anger, to make angry, to bring one along to a deep seated anger."[7] This kind of anger in children springs from continual and habitual unfair treatment. Wouldn't that kind of treatment make you angry? Of course it would. Some of you know exactly what I'm talking about because that's how your father treated you—and that's why you've struggled with bitterness and resentment toward him for so many years. I'm sure you don't want to repeat that kind of behavior with your kids. It may not have fouled up your sexual identity, but unless I miss my guess, it sure has put a damper on your life.

Habitual unfairness over the years results in an accumulation of anger that eventually embitters children toward their father. One commentator describes it this way: "A child frequently irritated by overseverity or injustice, to which, nevertheless, it must submit, acquires a spirit of sullen resignation, leading to despair."[8] What a terrible way to grow up!

William Hendriksen suggests there are at least six ways a father can embitter his children.[9]

1. *By over-protection.* This may be the most effective way in the world to feminize a young boy. I have stacks of articles that substantiate this fact but I won't bore you with them. Let me try to explain how this works in simple terms.

Little boys are aggressive because in the seventh or eighth week in the womb there is an explosion of the potent male hormone called testosterone. If that neurophysiological explosion in the developing brain does not take place, that child will be a girl. Testosterone makes little boys aggressive. It's part of being a male.

Stephen Clark writes: "The results of the many studies of aggression in men and women are strikingly consistent. In nearly all the studies, the male of the human species appears more aggressive than the female . . . the evidence could hardly be stronger that men are more aggressive than women. In fact, there is greater consensus among psychologists about this conclusion than about any other social, emotional, or intellectual difference between men and women."[10]

The worst thing you can do for a little boy is to overprotect him. Little boys do foolish things that are aggressive. They have not developed the wisdom that matures their divine orientation to aggression. They jump off the top of slides instead of sliding down them. They climb the rafters in the garage, hang onto a rope, and swing between them like Tarzan. When they slip and fall on the concrete, they split open their heads. That's part of being a little boy. It's a miracle of God that any boy lives long enough to become a man.

When I was eight, I climbed with my dad to the top of a massive rock overlooking the Yosemite Valley. A small brass rail stood between where I was standing with my dad and the valley four thousand feet below. On impulse, just for the fun of it, I grabbed the rail and swung my body out over the four-thousand-foot drop. If my hands had slipped, it would have been curtains. My dad looked over just as I was fully extended out over the valley. As I swung back toward the rock, he grabbed me and pulled me in. I knew I was in major trouble. He immediately took steps on my posterior to channel my aggressiveness in the future. I should have told him the testosterone made me do it.

We can damage our young boys by overprotecting them and by creating fear that they may get hurt. Little boys who are constantly overprotected are in jeopardy of having their masculinity warped. Obviously, we are to teach them to use good judgment. But we are not to squelch their aggressiveness. They will survive the scars and broken bones of boyhood. But they cannot survive being feminized through the perpetual fear of getting hurt. God made boys to be aggressive. We are to accept it and channel it.

2. *By favoritism.* If you don't think favoritism can embitter a child, go rent the movie video *Ordinary People.* That's all I need to say on this one.

3. *By discouragement.* Habitual messages from fathers to children like, "You'll never amount to any-

thing," or "Can't you do anything right?" can plague children for the rest of their lives. This is one of the easiest ways to embitter a child without realizing what you're doing. It can easily become a habit we are unaware of . . . a deadly habit.

4. *By forgetting that the child is growing up, has a right to have ideas of his own, and need not be an exact copy of his father.* If you want a clone of yourself, put your face on the Xerox machine and run off a few copies. But let your kids be themselves.

5. *By neglect.* Robert Coles hits the nail on the head on this one: "I think that what children in the United States desperately need is a moral purpose. They're getting parents who are very concerned about getting them into the right colleges, buying the best clothing for them, giving them an opportunity to live in neighborhoods where they'll lead fine and affluent lives and where they can be given the best toys, go on interesting vacations, and all sorts of things . . . Parents work very hard these days; and they're acquiring things that they feel are important for their children. And yet vastly more important things are not happening. *They're not spending time with their children*, at least not very much."[11]

I went to high school with quite a demographic cross-section. Most of us were middle-class. Although we had some very poor classmates in our school, some of my other classmates came from the wealthiest families in America. At the time, it amazed me that so many of my overtly wealthy friends were so embittered toward their parents. Now I know why.

6. *By bitter words and outright physical cruelty.* Kay Marshall Strom is right: "It's hard to comprehend

the life of children raised in an atmosphere of violence. Very early they learn that their home is different. They see that their friends' families are not like their own. Nor are television families or the ones they read about in their schoolbooks. They don't want to have their friends over. They can't look forward to weekends and holidays and vacations like other children do, because those are the times the abuse is likely to be worst.

"Confused and worried, these children desperately need to share their hurts with someone. Yet they are too afraid and too ashamed to talk about it. In time the wounds of violence heal, but the scars remain forever."[12]

Most men are abusive because they were abused. If that is your situation, I encourage you to break the chain. There are trained counselors who can help you. It will take some courage to admit your problem, but the generations to come will benefit from your willingness to admit your weakness.

Moral Landmark #2:
Fathers Should Raise
Their Children with Tenderness

The word translated in Ephesians 6:4 as "bring them up" means "to nourish, to provide for with tender care."[13] Masculine men are tender men. As we will see in a minute, this does not mean they cease being strong with their children. It just means they have a balance.

Children can quickly become embittered toward fathers when tenderness is missing. Just exactly what is tenderness? It's a sensitivity toward others. Allow me to let you in on a secret. It's easier for me to define tenderness than to practice it. This is a weakness of mine. Tenderness does not come naturally to me. Some people are tender by personality and temperament. I am not. It is something I am in the process of learning.

This weakness greatly concerns me, for if I allow it to go unchecked, I may end up embittering my children. That's why I work on it every day of my life. Unfortunately, I'm not alone in this weakness—a lot of you share it with me. So why don't we take a closer look at it?

Tenderness has different facets like a carefully cut diamond. If you look at tenderness from one angle, you'll see sympathy. If you look from another, you'll notice compassion. Tenderness also carries the ideas of responsiveness, warmth, and kindness.

Our children need to feel these things from us as well as from our wives. Our boys and girls need dads who are tuned in to them. They need dads who are interested in the stuff of their lives. *They need dads who will listen before they spank*. They need dads who will give them plenty of hugs and kisses. Recently, Lindsay Crosby, 51, the youngest of Bing Crosby's four sons from his first marriage, died of a self-inflicted gunshot wound. At one point, he was quoted as saying about his relationship with his father, "I never expected affection from my father so it didn't bother me." Perhaps it bothered him more than he realized.

Children also need dads who are kind. Every once in awhile, Mary will look at me and say, "Steve, you are not being kind." She has been right every time she has said it. As a result, I've tried to keep in mind the wise words of Allan Loy McGinnis: "Relationships are built up, like a fine lacquer finish, with the layers of kindness."

It is especially important that fathers be tender toward their daughters. A man who does not convey acceptance, warmth, tenderness, and compassion can easily embitter his daughter deeply. Dr. Peter Blitchington writes:

> Fathers play a strong role in their daughters' future sexual adjustment. Women who had a strong, stable relationship with a loving father usually find the adjustment to mature femininity much easier. They are usually more secure in their sexual nature and they find it easier to love their husbands.
>
> Fathers also strongly influence their daughters' future capacity to enjoy sexual relationships in marriage. The by-now-classic studies conducted at the Institute of Sexual Research consistently found that women whose fathers had been the dominant figure in the home and who had enjoyed a strong, stable relationship with their fathers were better able to achieve orgasm during sexual intercourse than women whose fathers were either passive or undependable. Thus, in order to enjoy sexual relationships, a woman needs to have experienced a stable relationship with her father; she needs to feel that men can be depended upon and trusted in order to be able to let herself go during the act of intercourse.[14]

If a young girl has a warm, loving, and tender relationship with her father, she will not bring into marriage the deeply embedded feelings of alienation that afflict young women without such dads. She will intuitively believe and expect her husband to treat her in a tender way just as her father treated her. She will look to marry a man with the same positive, tender characteristics she enjoyed with her father.

Boys must be raised in the same way. They must experience this same warmth, tenderness, and affection. When a boy is embittered by a father without a gentle and understanding side, the effects can be devastating. When a boy has a father who has modeled tenderness, it will be much easier for that boy to give the same tenderness and understanding to his children when he becomes a father.

One wise man wrote: "Many a young woman who opts for immoral sexual relationships does so because she can scarcely remember a time when her father so much as touched her. Unaffectionate dads, without ever wishing to do so, can trigger a daughter's promiscuity. All this leads me to write with a great deal of passion, dads, don't hold back your affection. Demonstrate your feelings of love and acceptance to both sons and daughters. And don't stop once they reach adolescence. They long for your affirmation and appreciation. They will love you for it. More importantly, they will emulate your example when God gives them their own family."[15]

Let me suggest four tips that can help a man develop tenderness with his children.

1. *Listen to them and respect their feelings.*

2. *If you have been wrong or too harsh with them, be man enough to clearly confess and admit your wrongdoing and ask their forgiveness.*

Don't make excuses; make a confession. Corrie Ten Boom once said, "The blood of Jesus never cleansed an excuse." Don't say, "I'm sorry if I was wrong," say "I was wrong. It was my fault." Spell it out with a repentant heart, and they will not only respect you, they will grow in their love for you.

About six months ago, I blew up at Rachel just before bedtime. Actually, I blew up about forty-five minutes after she was supposed to be in bed. It had been a long day, and I was extremely tired. For some reason, it seemed she kept lingering and hovering around the house. I wanted peace and quiet. Finally, Mount St. Helens blew. I'm sure the neighbors wondered what had so angered me. I told Rachel that she had fifteen seconds to be in bed—I repeat, *in* her bed.

She went to bed crying as the hot lava of my wrath pursued her up the stairs. After I came back down, Mary told me there were several good reasons she had been up. Some special event was to take place at school the next morning, and Rachel was getting ready for it. She wasn't lingering, she was preparing.

If I had bothered to ask Rachel what was going on, I could have discovered that for myself. But I didn't. I just vented on her. I made my way back up the stairs (careful not to step in the remaining pools of lava) and asked her forgiveness. I felt like a real jerk. We prayed together, and I tucked her in and decided the safest place for me was in bed as well. I told Mary I was turning in.

But I couldn't drop off to sleep. My explosion had unsettled me, too. I kept thinking of the enormous damage I could inflict on my exquisite ten-year-old daughter without even realizing it. The last thing I wanted to do was to crush her delicate spirit. Although we had patched it up and she had forgiven me, I couldn't get her off my mind.

After an hour or so, I got up, got in the car, and drove down to the twenty-four-hour supermarket. I found a red rose in a nice little vase, a card with a man peering out of a doghouse, and headed home. I wrote Rachel a note telling her that I really did love her and that I really was wrong. Then I placed the rose and the card on the kitchen table. It was the first thing she saw when she walked into the kitchen.

I figured after ruining her evening, the least I could do would be to make her day. It was worth the late-night trip. Instead of going off to school with memories of the red hot lava, she could think of her red, serene rose . . . and a dad who was genuinely sorry.

3. *Listen to the input your wife gives you about each child.* Usually she is more in tune with their emotional needs than you are. She can be a tremendous resource—but you have to listen to her.

4. *Be "high touch" and dispense liberal doses of encouragement to both sons and daughters (and don't forget your wife while you're at it).*

Moral Landmark #3:
Fathers Should Raise
Their Children with Firmness

Ephesians 6:4 says children are to be raised in the discipline and admonition of the Lord. The word *discipline* "may be described as training by means of rules and regulations, rewards, and when necessary, punishments. It refers primarily to *what is done to the child.*"[16]

By contrast, the word *admonition* is primarily "training by means of the spoken word, whether that word be teaching, warning, or encouragement. It refers primarily to *what is said to the child.*"[17]

The purpose of this discipline and admonition is to build the child. Children need to know what the limitations are. They need fathers who love them enough to set boundaries and keep them. Children need fathers who are in control. Quite frankly, there are too many families in America where the children are in control.

A number of years ago, a member of the Royal Family visited America for the first time. Upon returning to London after the lengthy visit, a reporter asked him to name the most amazing thing he saw in America. Without hesitation, he said, "The way the parents obey their children."

Kenneth Taylor, author of the *Living Bible* and the father of ten children, writes from a world of experience: "A father's task is many-sided, but the most important part of his work is to fit himself and his children into God's plan of family authority. Children are to be encouraged by the father's pat on the back and helped to better things when necessary by the application of the hand or stick to the seat of learning. Of course there are other methods of discipline besides spanking, but whatever is called for must be used. To refuse to discipline a child is to refuse a clear demand of God, for a child who doesn't learn to obey both parents will find it much harder to learn to obey God."[18]

Let me ask you a question. Do you take the lead in matters of discipline in the home, or do you leave it to your wife? According to Ephesians 6:4, it is clearly *your* responsibility. That doesn't mean, of course, that your wife doesn't discipline the children. But it does mean you are the one that sets the standards, enforces the standards, models the standards, and appropriately disciplines when the standards are violated.

Although you take the lead in disciplining the children, make sure you never undercut the discipline your wife takes in your absence. You are a team. Your kids need to see you support her actions. It will not only undergird the notion that you work in tandem, it will cause them to grow in their respect of your wife. When they see that you respect her decisions about discipline, they will respect her as well. And your support will relieve her of immeasurable pressure.

One more question. Who is in control at your house? You or your kids? How would your kids answer that? It may surprise you that some parents allow their children to have control as early as two and three months. That is a major mistake.

Balancing Tenderness with Firmness

Some men have a problem with being too firm and not being tender enough. Others have a problem with being too tender and not firm enough. Fathers are to be firm at times and flexible and tender at other times. It takes the wisdom of God to know which is appropriate. The good news is that He will give you wisdom, for Ephesians 6:4 instructs us to be ready to do one or the other at the appropriate time. But you, as the head, are always to control and lead your children. That is so important to God that a man who does not manage his own home well is not eligible for leadership in the church (1 Timothy 3:4,5).

There is a balance between firmness and tenderness that good fathers constantly try to achieve. Most of us tend to err on one side or the other. But we must strive to maintain that balance for the sake of our children. Don't get discouraged in your attempts to find the balance. Hang in there. For when you stop to think about it, there is only one way to achieve balance. We find balance by losing it.

Moral Landmark #4:
Fathers Should Raise Their Children in Christ

The phrase "in the discipline and instruction *of the Lord*" refers to the *quality* of training in the home. This is what ensures quality control. Discipline and admonition that are not "of the Lord" can quickly degenerate to verbal or physical abuse. That kind of behavior obviously does not meet the standards of Christ.

When a father disciplines and instructs his children in the admonition of the Lord, he is under the quality control of the Holy Spirit. His primary purpose is to train the child, not abuse the child. The fact that he is under the influence of this quality control—rather than out of control—is in and of itself an example to his children of the way they are to handle their children when they become parents. This quality control is to be modeled so that it can be imitated by the next generation.

Dave Simmons sums up our findings in Ephesians 6:

Fathers help boys develop strong healthy masculinity when the boys perceive them as the one who sets limits, makes decisions, controls disbursements of family capital, and administers discipline. Caution: these functions need to be undergirded with consistent affection and care-giving . . .

Fathers help girls develop strong healthy femininity by the above actions combined with personal intimacy and non-sexual physical contact. When the daughters receive the esteem-building attention and intimacy with dad, they learn to feel comfortable with masculinity and will relate well to their male peers, pick a good husband and be a good mother to a son.[19]

The Result of Reading a Properly Calibrated Compass

What results when a son reads the moral compass of his father and gets the correct moral bearings? What happens when a daughter has a father who provides the necessary reference points of fairness, tenderness, firmness—all under the quality control of Christ? *The result is a child who not only has a clear sexual identity but also has a backpack chock-full of healthy self-confidence.*

In his excellent book *Sex Roles and the Christian Family,* Dr. Peter Blitchington cites the results of a study done on children with high levels of self-esteem and self-confidence. Blitchington summarizes the study like this:

Parents of highly self-confident children met three criteria: First, they were very warm and accepting of their children. They showed in every way that they genuinely liked their children. Second, they provided clear guidance for their children. They laid down specific rules and regulations, and they expected their children to adhere to those guidelines. Third, they were respectful of their children's initiative and endeavors. They didn't stifle their children whenever they showed independent actions. So this research shows what Christians have known all along, that the best homes are those in which the parents combine love with strong guidance and clear values. In those homes the children will grow up to be self-confident and effective adults.[20]

A child with a clear sexual identity and a liberal amount of self-confidence will not be afraid or anxious of assuming the role of husband or wife when the proper time comes. Such children will know who they are and what they are to do in establishing a home.

In America, this type of young person is quickly becoming an endangered species. As more and more children are confused about who they are sexually, they naturally struggle with a lack of confidence because they don't know who they are or what they are to do. Masculinity or femininity has never been modeled for them.

Children who come from homes with accurate moral compasses will be clear as to who they are and what they are to do. A young man with a healthy compass, and a young woman with a healthy compass, will not lack for direction when they get married. Their goals and objectives will be clear, and they will be confident they can meet them. They will have very little anxiety about the new responsibilities that will soon be theirs when children come into their lives. They will not only choose to have children, but they will intuitively provide for them the same fairness, tenderness, and firmness they received while growing up.

The result? Another generation of children influenced for Christ. And that's what you call quality control.

Telling Your Kids What You Don't Want to Tell Them

There are some who are men and women at the age of sixteen, who have nothing more to learn about the erotic.

Allan Bloom

The photographer for a national magazine was assigned to get photos of a great forest fire. Smoke at the scene hampered him, and he frantically called his home office to hire a plane. "It will be waiting for you at the airport!" he was assured by his editor.

As soon as he got to the small, rural airport, sure enough, a plane was warming up near the runway. He jumped in with his equipment and yelled, "Let's go! Let's go!" The pilot swung the plane into the wind and soon they were in the air.

"Fly over the north side of the fire," said the photographer, "and make three or four low, level passes."

"Why?" asked the pilot.

"Because I'm going to take pictures!" said the photographer with great exasperation. "I'm a photographer, and photographers take pictures!"

After a long pause the pilot said, "You mean you're not the instructor?"

Guess what? When it comes to teaching your kids about sex, you are the instructor. That's the premise of this chapter. It's your responsibility to teach them the fundamentals of sexuality and how everything "works." It is essential, especially in our culture, that children get their information about sex from their parents. The reason it is so essential is that there are quite a few others who want the job.

In his book, *Grand Illusions: The Legacy of Planned Parenthood*, George Grant describes an interview with a young girl who sat through a "Health" class at her school:

> She tells the story of second period Tuesdays and Thursdays. It was "Health" class. This week, a representative of Planned Parenthood had come to talk about sex, contraception, pregnancy and abortion.

> "At first, I couldn't tell where all this was leading," Catherine said. "But then it became really obvious. She (the woman from Planned Parenthood) started asking us personal questions—very personal questions. Like about our feelings, about sex, and even about—well, about masturbation. It was so

224

disgusting. All the boys were kind of giggling but you could tell that even they were embarrassed. Then she showed us a film that was extremely explicit."

An unashamedly brash couple fondled one another in preparation for intercourse. At an appropriate moment of interest, the camera zoomed in for close-up shots—sweaty body parts rubbing, caressing, kissing, stroking, petting, embracing. At the height of passion, the camera fixed on the woman's hands, trembling as she tore open a condom package, and began to slowly unroll its contents onto her partner.

When the lights came back on, the entire class was visibly shaken. With eyes as wide as saucers, the youngsters sat speechless and amazed.

But their guest was entirely non-plussed.

"She began to tell us that everything we had just seen was totally normal and totally good. She said that the loving couple obviously had a caring, loving, and responsible relationship—because they took proper precautions against conception and disease."

At that, the teacher passed several packages around the room—one for each of the girls. She instructed the boys to hold up a finger so that the girls could practice contraceptive application.

Already shell-shocked, the students did as they were told.

Afterwards, several of the girls began quietly sobbing; another ran out of the room and threw up; still another fainted. Mercifully, the class ended just a moment later.

Catherine closed her interview by saying: "I have never been more humiliated in my life. I felt dirty and defiled after seeing the film. But then, when I had to put that thing on Billy's finger—well, that was just awful. It was horrible. It was like I'd been raped. Raped in my mind. Raped by my school. Raped by Planned Parenthood. I think I was—that we have all been betrayed."[1]

I'll give you a moment to recover from what you just read. Can you imagine that such a thing actually happened in a public school in this country? Remember that our children cannot pray in our schools, they cannot read the Bible in our schools, and the Ten Commandments cannot be posted in our schools, but when it comes to teaching morality (and that's precisely what sex education is), then suddenly there is an open door policy to godless influences like Planned Parenthood.

Tom Minnery writes the following enlightening words: "Across the country, local school districts are mandating abstinence as the basis of sex education. Sensing the trend, Planned Parenthood also offers the concept. But it defines abstinence as 'non-penetration'—everything else is OK."[2]

So Planned Parenthood officially endorses abstinence. But according to them, abstinence is "non-penetration."

Let me get this straight. If a teenage boy and girl

are involved in oral sex, then according to Planned Parenthood, they can truthfully say they are abstaining.

I like what that great theologian, Woody Allen, once said about abstinence: "I'd like to say just a word about oral contraception. I was involved in a very good example of oral contraception. I asked a girl to go to bed with me and she said, 'No.'"

On the surface, it appears that both Christians and Planned Parenthood agree that abstinence is a good thing. Yet, when you look at the definition, Planned Parenthood has something else in mind entirely. H. W. Shaw once said, "I have seen hypocrisy that was so artful it was good judgment to be deceived by it." That describes the situation here to the T.

Let's put the cards on the table. A war is raging for our children, and Planned Parenthood and its philosophical cousins are the enemy. They are trying to rip apart everything that remains that is right, moral, godly, and decent. And they are walking into our public schools every day with the intention of undercutting the value system of Christian parents.

In this chapter, I want to suggest a premise, a policy, and a procedure for teaching our children the truth about sexuality. In light of what our kids are getting in school, in the media, and from their friends, we have no choice but to educate them about the truth of God's gift of sex.

Maybe the thought of talking to your son about sex embarrasses you. Allow me to suggest that although you may feel some embarrassment, there is nothing to be embarrassed about. As Dr. Howard Hendricks expresses it: "We should not be ashamed to discuss that which God was not ashamed to create."

You cannot afford *not* to educate your children about sex. Yet the majority fail just here: ". . . Sex education is ignored by most parents, both Christian and non-Christian, out of discomfort, ignorance, or indifference. According to surveys, most adolescents report they have never been given any advice about sex by either parent. In another study, only about one-third of the adolescents surveyed reported that they had 'good talks with my parents about sex.'"[3]

I'm convinced that the reason most people don't educate their children about sex is that their parents did not educate them. As a result, sexual ignorance is passed from generation to generation. It's time to put a new link in the generational chain. If you teach your kids about sex, they will teach their kids, and their kids will teach theirs, and so on down the line.

The Premise of Parental Sex Education

I've already stated my premise elsewhere, but let me make it crystal clear. *A man is responsible to teach his children about sex.* As a rule of thumb, fathers should teach their sons and mothers should teach their daughters. But the father, as head of the family, has a responsibility to make sure that each child is given the proper and correct instruction by the appropriate parent at the right time.

The Book of Proverbs fits into a category known as wisdom literature. We tend to forget that Proverbs is a book. Our tendency is to break it up into little pieces and pull out the individual proverbs. But Proverbs, like every other book in the Bible, has a specific author writing with a specific purpose in mind. The primary author and purpose of Proverbs is stated in the opening six verses:

1 The proverbs of Solomon the son of David, king of Israel:

2 To know wisdom and instruction,
To discern the sayings of understanding,

3 To receive instruction in wise behavior,
Righteousness, justice and equity;

4 To give prudence to the naive,
To the youth knowledge and discretion,

5 A wise man will hear and increase in learning,
And a man of understanding will acquire wise counsel,

6 To understand a proverb and a figure,
The words of the wise and their riddles
(NASB).

Solomon's purpose in writing is to dispense wisdom. Solomon had a special gift of wisdom from God. Unfortunately, as his life progressed, he failed to implement much of what he wrote in this book. That does not negate the truth of his words.

Solomon wrote this book to his son. The Book of Proverbs is a father's instruction to a son, covering between fifty to eighty topics (depending on how you categorize the subjects).

One evening I read through Proverbs and circled every reference that specifically mentioned to whom Solomon was writing. In 1:8, he says "Hear, my son, your father's instruction" (NASB). In 2:1, Solomon writes, "My son, if you will receive my sayings . . ." (NASB). In 3:1, we read, "My son, do not forget my teaching." In chapter four, he addresses his son specifically three times, and so on throughout the book.

Proverbs is a book of teaching from father to son

about gaining wisdom for life. Someone has defined wisdom as "skill in everyday living." Sex is one of the main issues in the book. Solomon wants his son to have skill in knowing how to handle his sexuality. As we read through Proverbs, the topic of sex comes up time and time again.

As you read sections in Proverbs about sex, notice that the father is clear, direct, and takes the initiative. He describes sexual situations that probably will come up in his son's life, then offers the wisdom needed to handle the situation correctly. Solomon practiced preventive medicine. He wanted his son to know what steps to take in the event a tempting circumstance arose. Chapter 5 serves as an excellent example:

1 My son, give attention to my wisdom,
   Incline your ear to my understanding;

2 That you may observe discretion,
   And your lips may reserve knowledge.

3 For the lips of an adulteress drip honey,
   And smoother than oil is her speech;

4 But in the end she is bitter as wormwood,
   Sharp as a two-edged sword.

5 Her feet go down to death,
   Her steps lay hold of Sheol.

6 She does not ponder the path of life;
   Her ways are unstable, she does not know it.

7 Now then, my sons, listen to me,
   And do not depart from the words of my mouth.

8 Keep your way far from her,
   And do not go near the door of her house,

9 Lest you give your vigor to others,
And your years to the cruel one;

10 Lest strangers be filled with your strength,
And your hard-earned goods go to the house
of an alien;

11 And you groan at your latter end,
When your flesh and your body are consumed;

12 And you say, "How I have hated instruction!
And my heart spurned reproof!

13 "And I have not listened to the voice of my
teachers,
Nor inclined my ear to my instructors!

14 "I was almost in utter ruin
In the midst of the assembly and congregation."

15 Drink water from your own cistern,
And fresh water from your own well.

16 Should your springs be dispersed abroad,
Streams of water in the streets?

17 Let them be yours alone,
And not for strangers with you.

18 Let your fountain be blessed,
And rejoice in the wife of your youth.

19 As a loving hind and graceful doe,
Let her breasts satisfy you at all times;
Be exhilarated always with her love.

20 For why should you, my son, be exhilarated
with an adulteress,
And embrace the bosom of a foreigner?

21 For the ways of a man are before the eyes of
the Lord,
And He watches all his paths.

22 His own iniquities will capture the wicked,
   And he will be held with the cords of his sin.

23 He will die for lack of instruction,
   And in the greatness of his folly he will go
   astray (NASB).

Let's make three quick observations about Solomon's approach here in Proverbs 5. In verses 1-6, he tells his son about the kind of woman that will seek to bring him down. She is smooth with her words and extremely enticing. He warns his son about giving in to the impulse of immediate sexual indulgence. He also describes the true character of such a loose and promiscuous woman—what you see is *not* what you get.

In verses 7-14, he gets even more specific. He tells his son not to get near such a woman. He's to avoid going to her door at all costs. By avoiding her door, she cannot bring him down. In the remaining verses of this section he reiterates the consequences of becoming involved in adultery. He reminds his son of the great remorse that will follow the adulterous act. "Son," he says, "think about the consequences of your decision before you get into it. Don't do something stupid on impulse."

In the next paragraph, verses 15-23, he tells his son about the advantages of enjoying a pure sexual relationship in marriage. He tells him up front that he is to enjoy his wife sexually, and not to dispense his sexual energy to other women. He also reminds him that God is watching his behavior, and will severely discipline him if he violates the marriage covenant.

Proverbs 5 shows us that a father is to talk straight with his son about the boundaries God has put around his gift of sex. Notice that the father doesn't mince any words. He attempts to prepare his son for what might occur long before it happens. This is precisely what we are to do as leaders of our home.

If this was important in Solomon's day, how much more so in ours? Solomon was the king of Israel and could keep the Jerusalem chapter of Planned Parenthood out of the schools. We can't. It is even more incumbent upon us that we follow Solomon's lead, since our children are being raised in a culture that promotes and encourages sexual activity outside of marriage.

One of my goals for each of my children is that they be virgins when they get married. I don't think Planned Parenthood shares that goal. I want to do everything I can to encourage my kids to remain sexually pure until they walk into the church to be wed. That's a goal I have both for my daughter and for my two sons.

In our culture, the worst thing a single man can be called is a virgin. Virgin has become a derogatory term. But it's not derogatory, it's exemplary. In my opinion, the Boy Scouts ought to give a merit badge for virginity. Boys do *not* have to sow wild oats. That is a myth. What a boy needs to sow from his earliest years are the seeds that will enable him to enter marriage as a one-woman kind of man. He will only take that course, however, if he has a father who encourages him in that direction.

If you are a one-woman kind of man, you should be equipping your sons to enter the marriage covenant with sexual purity and truly be one-woman kind of men from the first day they are married. So much for our premise: *A man is responsible to teach his children about sex.* Now let's look at the policy.

The Policy of Parental Sex Education

The policy is easy to remember: *Get to your kids before their peers do!* That's it. The question is, at what age will their peers begin to bring up the issue?

I like the point Connie Marshner makes in her book, *Decent Exposure: How to Teach Your Kids About Sex.* Connie writes: ". . . if your child is ten years old and there has been no communication between the two of you about reproduction, sexuality, or male-female differences, there is no time to waste."[4]

Connie is exactly right; there is no time to waste. If your child is ten years old and doesn't know the scoop yet, get on the stick! If your child is ten, let me assure you that he knows more than you think he knows. He has already gotten the information. The only question is, from whom did he get it and how accurate is it?

Let's reiterate the policy: *Get to your kids before their peers do!* That means if you're going to err, err on the side of introducing the subject too early rather than too late. Remember, guys, *we* are to be the instructors of our children, not some kid on a playground. That means we must be tuned in to our kids. We must be alert for the subtle signals they send out that indicate big questions in their mind. Your wife can be a big help here. As June Cleaver used to say, "Ward, I'm worried about the Beaver."

It may be that you are in tune, but not getting any signals. That's okay. Maybe it hasn't crossed his mind yet. In my opinion, however, as a boy approaches the age of seven, a father should begin to think about an opportune time to speak with his son about sex. Your son may not be thinking about it, but I guarantee you that at least one of his friends is. The same approximate guideline can be used for mothers and daughters. Please understand that this is simply a guideline. This doesn't come from inerrant Scripture, it's only a suggestion.

In some cases, it may need to happen sooner; in others, a little later. If you ask the Holy Spirit to give you wisdom as to the best time for your child, He will give it to you. Don't feel pressured. Just be sensitive to your child and to the Lord. He'll let you know when it's time.

So far we have established the premise and the policy. Now let's talk about the procedure.

The Procedure for Parental Sex Education

One of his closest friends said that Winston Churchill spent a good part of his life rehearsing impromptu speeches. One day his valet, having drawn his master's bath shortly before, heard Churchill's voice booming out from the bathroom. The valet stuck his head in to find out if anything was needed. Churchill, immersed in the bathtub, said, "I was not speaking to you, Norman, I was addressing the House of Commons."[5]

When a man sits down to talk with his son, he should follow Churchill's example. You want to be impromptu, but you also want to be prepared. Let me offer eight suggestions that will give you guidelines as you prepare your impromptu session on sex, and also for the continuing discussions thereafter.

1. *Small questions deserve small answers.*

I heard about a little boy who approached his father after dinner and asked, "Daddy, where did I come from?" The father nearly choked with surprise, but managed to gather himself. Since they were alone in the den, he thought this would be as good a time as any, so he commenced to tell the boy about the sperm, the egg, and all of the pertinent information. After about five minutes, he looked at his son's blank stare and asked, "Son, is this making any sense?" The boy replied, "I guess so, Dad, but Tommy came from Cleveland. Where do we come from?"

Make sure you understand the question before you commence with an answer.

2. *Big questions deserve big answers.*

The other night as I was watching the news and John was reading a book, he overheard the newscaster's story and said, "Dad, what is AIDS anyway?" That's what you call a big question. It got a big answer. Up to that point in his life, John did not know about homosexuality. After our discussion, he did know about it. And he was shocked.

When I told him there were men who had sex with other men, he could not believe his ears. I was sorry he had to hear about it at all. But I wanted him to hear it from me, and not someone else. I also told him that except for a few tragic situations where someone has gotten AIDS from a blood transfusion, that if he and his wife would obey what God says about sex, he would never get AIDS. He was very glad to hear that.

3. *Frank questions deserve frank answers.*

Several weeks ago, John came running upstairs and said, "Dad, I've got to ask you a question." I said,

"Okay, shoot." He said, "It's private." I said, "Okay," dropped what I was doing (which was writing this book), and John shut the door.

He said, "Dad, if a couple gets married, and then gets divorced, and then later they decide that it was a mistake to get a divorce and they get married again, would they have sex again?"

I have no idea where that question came from. But it was something John was trying to figure out. He asked me a frank question, and I gave him a frank answer. I said, "Yes." He thought for a second, and said, "Okay, thanks, Dad," and went back downstairs to play with his Legos.

Regardless of how well you think you are explaining everything, a boy of that age has not put all the pieces together. It's sort of like playing with Legos. You can give your kids all of the pieces and explain each piece as carefully as possible, but it will take a child several years to be able to coordinate all of those pieces.

John wanted to know if a divorced couple who got remarried would want to have sex again. You and I know the obvious answer. He didn't. Like any young boy, he's still putting the pieces together.

It's like what a friend of mine told several of us awhile back. He has three children and was explaining the facts of life to his seven-year-old son. When he told his son that babies came from sexual intercourse and proceeded to explain what that was, his boy got an astonished expression on his face and said, "You mean that you and Mom have done that three times?"

4. *Be casual and natural.*

The reason for this is simple. If you're tense and nervous about discussing it, you're going to make your children tense and nervous. The fact of the matter is that there is nothing to be tense about.

You want to create an environment for your children that makes them feel the most natural thing in the world is to ask Dad and Mom their questions about sex. So be casual and natural. Be relaxed. Even if you're tense on the inside and you have to chew two or three packs of Tums afterwards, don't let on that you're tense. Be cool. Chill out. Defrost, if necessary. Whatever you do, create an atmosphere where they feel comfortable in coming to you. If you don't, they will go to someone else. And that, my friend, is something to get tense and nervous about.

5. *Look for teachable moments.*

You never know when a teachable moment is going to show up. When one does, make sure you teach. A teachable moment is a special time or circumstance that ignites an unusual teachability in your child. Take full advantage of these times. They are gifts from God.

Josh McDowell relates a teachable moment that happened with his kids. His wife was unable to pick him up at the airport, so his secretary came to get him with his two oldest children. As they were driving home, his kids got in an argument. "F___ you!" said his son to his sister.

What would you do in that situation? Listen to how McDowell turned that into a teachable moment:

> Sean obviously didn't know what the word meant. If I had jumped on him and told him how dirty the word was, he would have learned not only that the word was bad, but he would also have a negative impression

about the sex act itself when he learned what it was.

So instead I said, "Son, where did you learn that word?"

"On the school bus," he answered.

"Do you know what it means?" I asked.

"No."

"Can I explain it to you, then?"

"Yeah!" he answered. "What is it?" He was dying to know.

And for the next forty minutes, I had a fabulous opportunity to teach my son and daughter about the sanctity, the beauty, and the purpose of sex. It was an opportunity for which I was extremely grateful, an experience I'll never forget—nor I suspect will they.[6]

Note that Josh created a teachable moment out of what might have been an explosive one instead. He had the wisdom in that situation not to react but to teach.

St. Francis Xavier once said, "Give me the children until they are seven and anyone may have them afterwards." That's true if you'll capture the teachable moments.

6. *Use the right terms without embarrassment.*

Sometimes this is tough to do. It's not that you will be embarrassed for using the right terms, but that your kids will embarrass you when they know the right terms. Some friends of ours are very good parents, and have been careful to use the right terminology with their children.

One day while grocery shopping, the mother walked thirty or forty feet away from the cart, past the crowds of people, looking for a specific item. Suddenly her little three-year-old, sitting in the cart, yelled out with great excitement, "Hey, Mom, look! I've got an erection!"

Sometimes it's tough when your kids know the right terms. But the thing about kids is that they can embarrass you even when they don't know the right terms. So go ahead and tell them the right terms. You may have to change grocery stores, but that's okay.

7. *Consider the age of the child.*

We have already touched on this issue, but to underscore our previous remarks, remember that you are going to give a five-year-old a different answer to the same question than you are a nine-year-old.

8. *Let them know that they can ask you anything and get a straight answer.*

This is the cardinal doctrine of parental sex education. If you establish this, it doesn't matter what they hear somewhere else, for they will come to you for clarification. At certain points you may have to swallow hard before you answer, but whatever you do, don't skirt the issue. Deal with it head on. This kind of honest dialogue will be the greatest investment you will ever make. It will pay dividends in your relationship for the rest of your lives.

From time to time, I'll be in a conversation with a group of men, and this subject will come up. Inevitably, men express their frustration about knowing exactly what to say to their sons. They know they should say *something*, but they are not sure how to go about it. They didn't hear it from their dads growing up and therefore don't have a model to work from.

If you are clued into the eight principles above, you will create an environment for your children where it is natural to talk with you about sex. But perhaps until now it's been a closed issue in your home. In reading this chapter and realizing the ages of your children, perhaps you're coming to the conclusion that it's time for you to do some educating. What do you do now and how do you say it?

I am certainly no expert. But let me relate to you the essence of a conversation I had last year with John. John was seven, and I had been thinking about this for several months. I had been monitoring his dialogue with his friends, and I concluded that we needed to talk if I was going to get to my son before his peers did.

John and I had a private talk one night after dinner. Because it was confidential, I went to John the other day and asked him if it would be okay for me to relate in this chapter some of our talk that evening. He thought it would be a good idea.

"You know, Dad," he said, "it might help some kids learn about sex and keep them from getting into trouble. If dads would tell their kids about it, it would mean a lot to their kids."

I offer what follows not as a "how-to," but as a reference that might be helpful as you think through your own "impromptu" talk with your child.

A Personal Experience

John and I had spoken informally about sex before. He would ask a small question, and I would give him a small answer. But John had just turned seven, and things were changing in his world.

After dinner one evening, I decided it was time. We went up to his room and I said, "John, have you ever wondered how God makes babies?"

He said, "Yeah, Dad, I have."

"Well, John, I want to talk with you about that because that is a very special thing God invented. John, I'm going to tell you some things tonight you are not going to believe. But before I tell you about this, I want you to understand that it is a great thing and that it was God who created it. It's something he has given to dads and moms that is very, very good. I want to tell you about God's gift of sex. What do you know about sex, John?"

Several weeks earlier, he had told me about a junior high girl down the street who had "sexed." It was clear at that point he had no clue what that meant. But it told me that the subject was beginning to be a matter of discussion.

John said, "I know that girl down the street sexed with some boys."

I said, "John, it is very important for you to understand that God has said sex is something for moms and dads only. God says that we are to have sex only when we are married. But some people who aren't married still have sex."

"Really?"

"Yes, they really will. And they shouldn't because they are misusing the gift God has given, and that isn't right. People disobey God when they have sex and they are not married. But God is pleased when mommies and daddies have sex because they are married."

I started this way because I wanted to lay a foundation. I wanted him to know that sex came from God. I also wanted him to know that sex was a gift from God, but that God was very clear about how we were to enjoy his gift. This prevented him from getting the idea that sex was wrong or dirty.

Then it was time to go for it. I said, "Now, John, here is the part that you aren't going to believe. This is so wild you aren't going to believe it. But it's true. Let me tell you how this works. When a husband and wife have sex, you know what they do? They take all their clothes off. They get completely naked. And then they get in bed.

"This is when something happens to the daddy's penis. It gets real strong and big. That's called an erection."

Then I said, "John, do you know little girls don't have a penis? Well, they have what is called a vagina. And that's how God made girls. Boys have a penis, and girls have a vagina. When a mommy and daddy have sex, the daddy puts his erect penis inside the mommy's vagina."

I should mention at this point, that the eyes were as big silver dollars and the face carried an expression of complete unbelief (I don't mean John's face, I mean my own. I couldn't believe I was telling this to a seven-year-old.)

I said, "John, can you believe that? Isn't that wild?"

He said, "That's unbelievable, Dad!"

Then I said, "What happens is that this stuff called semen comes out of the daddy's penis and goes into the mommy's vagina. The daddy's semen has inside of it little things called sperm. There are millions of them. They are so small you can't see a thing without a microscope. Inside the mommy are all of these little eggs which are almost as small. And when a sperm finds an egg and they come together, that's what God uses to make a baby."

I was trying to simplify this as much as possible so that he could get a basic idea of what was happening. You want to use the correct terms but you want to make your explanation as simple as possible.

"Now, John," I continued, "I know that is really hard to understand right now, but I want you to know that it is really neat. Moms and dads really enjoy that, and you will enjoy it with your wife. But remember, this is something so special, that God only wants mommies and daddies to do it with each other.

"John, as you grow up, you are going to have friends and guys in school say things to you about sex. Most of them don't know what they're talking about. The reason they don't know what they're talking about is that they haven't heard about it from their dads. I'm telling you stuff tonight that most seven-year-olds don't know. In fact, you know more about this than most of your friends.

"But I want you to understand something very important. If you hear something that you're not sure of, or if you have any question, and I mean *any*, you can come to me and I will tell you the truth. You don't have to be embarrassed because we can talk about anything. You don't need to ask your friends because they don't know. But if you come to me, I'll tell you the truth."

I wanted him to know that we have an open-door policy. Believe me, he uses it. I'm very glad he does.

Then I said, "John, what do you know about *Playboy* magazine?

He said, "Joey (not his real name; names have been changed to protect the innocent) down the street told me that his dad subscribes to *Playboy*."

"Have you ever seen it?"

"No, but Joey told me that it has pictures of naked ladies in it."

"John, one day one of your friends is going to want to show you a magazine like that. If you see a picture of a naked lady you're going to like it. But not everything that is appealing to us is good for us. There are all kinds of magazines that show all kinds of naked ladies doing all kinds of things. That's what is called pornography.

"And even though it's tempting to look at those magazines, it very important that you don't. It's very important, John, that you protect your mind. Let me ask you a question, and it's kind of a gross situation. If you were thirsty and you went to get a drink of water, and for some reason, the water wouldn't come out of the tap, would you walk over to the toilet and scoop some water out and drink it?"

"Dad, that's gross! I would never do that."

"I know you wouldn't, John, but that's what you do to your mind when you look at pornography. It's like putting toilet water in your mind. And you want to protect your mind. So when someone wants you to look at that stuff, be man enough to walk away.

They'll probably make fun of you. But you tell them that you're not going to drink toilet water. You're smarter than that."

What I was doing here was attempting to instill in him the principle of standing alone. I want my children to be strong enough to stand against the current of peer pressure. So I painted a probable situation, described how he should respond, described how they would respond, and then gave him something to say so that he would be prepared.

"John, some of those ladies in those pictures have very sad lives. Most of them come from homes where their dads didn't love them, and they're trying to get attention. Some of those ladies are drug addicts and let men take pictures of them naked so they can get money to buy drugs. But you know what, John, we ought to feel sorry for those ladies. They don't know Jesus and most of them have terrible family situations, if they even have a family. But every one of them is somebody's daughter, or sister, or mommy."

John was horrified that someone's mom or sister or daughter would do such a thing. When I put pornography in the context of family relationships, it put a different light on it for him. He also felt bad that some women would act like that to get money for drugs.

I was trying here, in advance, to give him a perspective on pornography before he comes across it. I was trying to give him a viewpoint on pornography that would offset its initial allure.

I'm glad I got to John before his peers did. Inevitably, when you have a talk like that, you are not only going to answer some questions, you will raise others. That's why I underscored the fact that he could ask me anything and I would give him a straight answer.

A few weeks later, we were shooting baskets after dinner, and he said, "Dad, I need to ask you a question." He had been thinking about some things, and we casually talked as we practiced our bank shots.

A couple of weeks later, he asked Mary about the eggs inside a mommy. John couldn't figure what would happen if those eggs cracked inside her. Now, his question made a lot of sense to me when I heard it. The only eggs John had ever seen were the ones in the refrigerator. Mary explained to him the difference. I was glad he felt that he could approach his mom to ask her a question about girls. In a healthy home, at various times, there will be appropriate input from mother to son and father to daughter.

It's been over a year since we had our talk. On average, I would say John asks me a question about sex every week or two. It's as natural for him to ask me about sex as it is to talk about football. That's the way it should be. Just the other day we were coming home from running some errands, and as we were getting out of the car, John said, "Dad, is sex fun?"

I said, "John, you can't believe how much fun it is."

Now John had a context to hear those words. He knows there are rules for sex that make it fun, just like there are rules for football that make it fun. If the other team gets five downs, that's no fun. Our kids need to hear from us that sex is positive, fun, and enjoyable within the boundaries God has set.

The key word in all of this discussion about sex is

not rules, it is relationship. Our children should know that there are rules, but they should learn about them only from the context of a relationship that is open, warm, and loving. I like Josh McDowell's word of advice: "Rules without relationship equal rebellion—either active resistance or passive indifference. If you really want to help your child say no to premarital sex, the most important thing for you to do is not to establish rules but to build a strong, loving relationship with your child."[7]

Go for It!

Good luck on preparing your impromptu talk. God will give you the wisdom you don't have. If you don't know the answer, say, "I don't know, but I'll find out and get back to you." Then find out and get back to your son.

Guys, this is our responsibility. Dads teach boys, moms teach girls. I think that's God's way. If you are uncomfortable with that idea, just think of the alternatives. Your son can hear about sex from a friend, or you could take him by Planned Parenthood and let them give it a whirl. They would be more than willing to educate your child for you.

That's why you need to do it. Ruth Smelter once said that "every child has the right to be well fed and well led." Let's go lead. Your loving leadership in this area is the greatest thing you can do to keep your child from becoming another statistic on teen sex research.

There are no guarantees, but the fact is that if you do your job in this area, you will greatly increase the chances of keeping your child from becoming a statistic. Without your help, there is a real chance your kids could become another number on the teen pregnancy charts, or the abortion reports, or on the latest findings on sexually active teenagers. With God's grace, our kids won't become statistics.

Paul Brodeur is right: "Human beings are statistics with the tears wiped off." If we start early enough, we can prevent a lot of broken hearts, fractured lives, and unnecessary tears.

CHAPTER ELEVEN

Rock and Role Model

Life must be understood backward, but it must be lived forward.

Søren Kierkegaard

There are seventy-six million baby boomers in the United States. I've been assuming in this book that you are one of them. You qualify as a baby boomer if you were born between the years of 1946 and 1964. We baby boomers are the parents of this generation. When you realize that we seventy-six million baby boomers now have at least fifty-four million children, that comes to a total of 130 million people. That means that half of the population of the United States is living in a baby boomer household.

I agree with Hans Finzel: "Baby boomers are taking over and running over America! . . . No longer just making noise on the sidelines, boomers are taking charge of the corporations, factories, organizations, schools and churches of our land. With this positioning comes influence, the power to change the way things are viewed and done."[1]

We have become the people of influence in America. The ball is in our court. When we were kids we would often get upset about the way our parents handled things. Now we are the parents, and we get to make the decisions. And the decisions we make with our power and influence will have a tremendous impact on the next generation.

We baby boomers are now in our late twenties, thirties, and forties. We are actually either in mid-life or fast approaching it. I am astonished that I am now officially middle-aged. The other day I was in a store, and a seventeen-year-old salesgirl pointed to me and said to another teenage employee, "Would you help that man with the gray hair?" That's how she pointed me out. Gray hair. At forty, I guess I should be grateful I have any hair at all.

The fact is we are now in the driver's seat. We are the decision makers of American culture as we press toward the new millennium. Yesterday, I picked up a news magazine and read an article about the financial prospects for the next ten years. I found a significant prediction:

> Pay for baby boomers won't beat inflation, except for those who get steady promotions. But as they reach their middle 40s, they'll start topping out in their careers. Expect a

national midlife crisis—studded with divorces, career changes and a search for satisfaction in family and community values outside of work.[2]

The author of that article is right: We're getting ready to hit a national midlife crisis. That's why I've written this book. We male baby boomers are entering a difficult period of our lives. We must come to grips with the fact that our youthfulness is vanishing with every passing day. Some of us are going to stall in our careers, others are going to be tempted to chuck our job, leave our families, buy a red Mazda Miata and a few gold chains, and try to cover our bald spots as we think about asking out the new twenty-three-year-old receptionist.

That's the kind of weird things guys do when they hit midlife. But we can't do that. We have an enormous responsibility to our families and to God to handle this transition with great wisdom and care.

A midlife crisis is hard to avoid and may be impossible to escape altogether. But there is something we can do to help us make the transition smoothly and keep us from making some stupid and foolish decisions.

If I could sum up the message of this book, I would put it simply. Gentlemen, if you are going to win the war for your family, you must do two things:

- You must be a rock.
- You must be a role model.

That's it. If we male baby boomers can fix those responsibilities in our minds and practice them faithfully, each of us can make a powerful contribution to

the lives of those we love the most and to the kingdom of God.

All you have to remember is rock and role. Now,
"rock 'n' roll" is part of being a baby boomer. We grew
up with it and watched it go from Elvis to the Beatles
to the Stones to the Beach Boys to Crosby, Stills and
Nash, to the Eagles. We know all about the
Temptations, the Supremes, the Who, and Simon and
Garfunkel. Rock 'n' roll deeply affected the baby boom
generation.

Rock and role modeling, on the other hand, must
be our effect on the next generation. God is looking
for men between twenty-five and forty-five who will
commit to be "rocks" for their families. These kind of
rocks are characterized by an unwavering commitment
to their wives, a willingness to get involved in the lives
of their children, and a gut-level desire to follow hard
after Jesus Christ. These rocks are willing to apply their
Christian principles to their careers, even if it costs
them a promotion. These rocks know that true success
is not measured by a man's net worth but by his willingness to "Seek ye first the kingdom of God, and His
righteousness, and all these things shall be added unto
you."

Now, it's not easy for a man to choose to be a
rock. Being a rock is tough—but it's necessary. It's easier for a man to become a rock if he had a father who
was one. All he has to do is emulate the example of
his father.

But what if your father wasn't a rock? If your dad
wasn't a rock, you didn't have a role model. That's
why "rock" and "role model" go hand in hand. A man
who's decided to be a rock has decided to be a role

model. When a man chooses not to be a rock, the role model splits, too.

If your father wasn't a rock in your life, have you ever wondered why? Usually, the answer is that he didn't have his own rock and role model. And why not? Probably because his dad didn't have a rock and role model. And on and on it goes.

What if your father was a rock and role model for you? Why was it that he provided such a positive model? The answer probably is that he had a rock and role model in his life that he emulated. And where did his dad learn how to be such a rock? He learned it from his father. And on and on it goes.

The point is this. An invisible chain links the generations. It is a rule of life that boys grow up to be like their fathers. And that can either be positive or negative.

What if the generational chain handed to you is negative? What if there hasn't been a rock and role model in your family for generations? Does that mean you are consigned to a life of repeating those negative links in the chain?

Absolutely not!

The good news is you can forge a new link in the chain. You can make a difference. You can make a conscious decision to become a rock and role model who will change your generational chain from a negative to a positive. The choices you make today will not only affect your children, but their children, and their children, and their children. One man can make a difference . . . one man who chooses to be a rock.

But how do you become a rock if you haven't

had a role model? That is where the good news comes in. If you know Jesus Christ personally, you have not only a rock, but a role model. And this rock and role model isn't just any old version—this One is perfect.

None of us have had perfect role models, and none of us will be perfect role models. There is only one perfect Father, and He is in control of the universe. He has a Son who is the exact representation of His nature, and we are called to emulate His Son. I want to say this reverently—I don't say it lightly—but every one of us must realize that Jesus Christ is our personal rock and our personal role model.

What a tremendous weight upon a child not to have a rock in his life! What a heavy load to bear for the child who grew up without a role model! Some of you know what it is to live under that kind of burden. You can identify with the little boy Judith Wallerstein describes in her book on the effects of divorce, *Second Chances*:

> When six-year-old John came to our center shortly after his parents' divorce, he would only mumble, "I don't know." He would not answer questions; he played games instead. First John hunted all over the playroom for the baby dolls. When he found a good number of them, he stood the baby dolls firmly on their feet and placed the miniature tables, chairs, beds, and eventually all the playhouse on their heads. Then, wordlessly, he placed all the mother dolls and father dolls in precarious positions on the steep roof of the dollhouse. As a father doll slid off the roof, John caught him and, looking up at

me, said, "He might die." Soon all the mother and father dolls began sliding off the roof. John caught them gently, one by one, saving each from falling to the ground.

"Are the babies the strongest?" I asked.

"Yes," John shouted excitedly. "The babies are holding up the world."[3]

What kind of father do you think this little six-year-old has? I don't know the boy's father, but I can tell you this: He is no rock and he is no role model.

The babies are not holding up the world—Jesus Christ is. And the man who chooses to make Jesus Christ the Rock and Role Model of his life will find that Christ will hold him up as well.

Jesus once spoke some powerful words that apply to those of us who want to lead our families:

"Therefore everyone who hears these words of Mine, and acts upon them, may be compared to a wise man, who built his house upon the rock.

"And the rain descended, and the floods came, and the winds blew, and burst against that house; and yet it did not fall, for it had been founded upon the rock.

"And everyone who hears these words of Mine, and does not act upon them, will be like a foolish man, who built his house upon the sand.

"And the rain descended, and the floods came, and the winds blew, and burst against that house; and it fell, and great was its fall."

The result was that when Jesus had finished these words, the multitudes were amazed at His teaching; For He was teaching them as one having authority, and not as their scribes (Matthew 7:24-29, NASB).

Jesus Christ is the Rock. Jesus Christ is the Role Model. The multitudes were amazed at Him. Why? Because He was a Role Model of a kind they had never seen.

Jesus Christ is looking for men in the baby boomer generation who have a desire to become rock and role models for this disintegrating generation. If you are willing to respond to the call of Christ, He will unleash the power of the Holy Spirit in your life to use you to hold up the world of your family. And as Christ empowers you to hold up your world, your children will not have to bear that burden.

It's a Herculean task to lead a family, but with the power of God supporting you, it is a tremendous privilege. If we are willing to become the point man in our families, we can count on God's support and power. He's looking for men who will follow Jesus Christ and burn their ships behind them. When He finds those men, He will take extraordinary measures to buttress, bolster, and carry them along in His limitless strength.

The eyes of the LORD move to and fro throughout the earth *that He may strongly support those* whose heart is completely His (2 Chronicles 16:9, NASB).

May we be those men! And may He give us the strength to withstand the onslaught of His blessing.

The Meaning of Headship in the New Testament

David Roper is one of my all-time favorite Bible teachers. When I was in seminary, I heard him tell the following story:

> A number of years ago I was with my family at a conference center. Carolyn and I were seated in the lodge waiting for dinner to be served. Right behind the lodge was an embankment which recently had been seeded. There were signs posted which said, KEEP OFF THE BANK. Two of our sons, who were then quite young, were playing at the top of the embankment.
>
> Suddenly the director of the conference, who was seated with us, jumped to his feet

and shouted, "Stay off the bank!" and ran out the door. To my horror, as I looked out the window, there was one of our boys poised right at the top of the bank. The director was shouting, "Get off! Get off the bank!" but down the bank the boy slid, right into his arms. The director shook him, "Son, didn't you hear me say, 'Stay off the bank'?"

Of course, I was mortified. I took him around the building, got out a little switch and worked him over. I kept saying, "Son, didn't you hear the man say, 'Stay off the bank'?" As we were walking back he looked up at me with tear-stained eyes and said, "Daddy, what's a bank?"[1]

That little guy had a rough experience because he didn't understand something that was so obvious to everyone else. Obviously, Dave felt terrible when he understood the problem. Dave knew what a bank was, and the conference director knew what it was, but his little boy didn't have a clue what it was.

There are several possible meanings for the word *bank*. Personally, I have fished off a bank, cashed a check at a bank, spent hours on a basketball court shooting bank shots, and assured someone else that I would keep a promise by saying, "You can bank on it."

Some folks who reject the idea that God has assigned men and women differing roles—that is, those in the "egalitarian" camp—have attempted to show that the Greek word translated "head" should rather be translated "source." If this is the case, then the husband is not primarily responsible to God for family decisions.

Dr. Wayne House points out the textual difficulty for such a view:

> Some feminists go to great lengths to argue that to be one's "head" means to be one's "source." Based on this, the text supposedly teaches that Christ is the source of man, the man is the source of the woman, and God is the source of Christ.

> The inescapable problem with this view, however, is that the meaning for "head" is questionable. There is no clear example of the Greek word for "head" meaning "source" during the times of the writing of the New Testament, nor is any example in the New Testament reasonably translated this way. It is a forced, artificial definition of a New Testament word, adopted to support a pre-determined interpretation.[2]

John Piper asks: "What is the meaning of 'head' in Ephesians 5:23? The Greek word 'head' (*kephale*) is used in the Old Testament sometimes to refer to a chief or leader." Piper goes on to point out "that Paul's own use of the word 'head' in Ephesians 1:22 unquestionably carries with it the idea of authority."[3] "Headship" means that in the marriage relationship, the husband has the God-ordained authority and primary responsibility to lead the family. In contemporary terms, the buck stops with him.

Another Scriptural support used by those in the egalitarian or "two-headed" camp is Galatians 3:28:

> There is neither Jew nor Greek, slave nor free, male nor female, for you are all one in Christ Jesus.

The context of this passage is critically important. The text here is not addressing the marriage relationship or how it is to function. It is not speaking about marriage at all. Some have gone to this passage to argue there is to be no captain or co-captain in the marriage relationship. They claim that this passage implies there are to be two captains in the marriage cockpit. They believe this text erases any differences between husbands and wives, differences that are clearly taught in other portions of the New Testament. The problem with such a conclusion is that the context demonstrates the verse has nothing to do with the subject of marriage.

None of us appreciate having our remarks taken out of context. I think it's only fair that we extend the same courtesy to Paul in his inspired remarks on Galatians 3:28.

What, then, is Paul saying in Galatians 3:28? James Hurley writes that ". . . within its context, Galatians 3:28 addresses the question, 'Who may become a son of God, and on what basis?' It answers that any person, regardless of race, sex, or civil status, may do so by faith in Christ . . . The gospel is for all persons."[4]

That was a radical teaching in Paul's day. Some today accuse Paul of trying to diminish the importance or status of women in the church, but nothing could be further from the truth. Just the opposite is true. A popular Jewish prayer was making the rounds during the era of the New Testament. It went like this:

> Blessed art thou, O Lord our God, King of the
> universe,
> who hast not made me a Gentile (heathen).

Blessed art thou, O Lord our God, King of the
universe,
who hast not made me a slave.
Blessed art thou, O Lord, our God, King of the
universe,
who hast not made me a woman.[5]

The thrust of this prayer was not a hatred or dis-
trust of women. Rather, it reflects the false notion that
only a male Jew who was not a slave could be a first-
class citizen in the kingdom of God. Galatians 3:28
attacks that conclusion like a pit bull going after a
mailman. Paul was refuting the religious discrimination
that had crept into the practice of the religious leaders
of his day. The apostle loudly declared that the gospel
was not just for male Jews who were free; the gospel
was, and is, for everyone. That is the point of
Galatians 3:28. *Paul was raising the status of women,
not diminishing it.*

Aristotle once said: "The female is a female by
virtue of a lack of certain qualities. We should regard
the female in nature as afflicted with natural defective-
ness." Hundreds of years later, Napoleon was reported
to have made the following comment: "Nature intended women to be our slaves, they are our property,
we are not theirs, they belong to us just as a tree that
bears fruit belongs to a gardener."

Neither of those statements, of course, even
comes close to reflecting the biblical teaching about
the role of women. Wherever Christianity has gone
throughout the world, the position of women has been
elevated and improved.

A Christian man views his wife with tremendous
respect, for she too is made in the image of God and

has access to the very throne room of God. But the husband has been appointed by God as the leader in the marriage relationship. He is the captain in the marriage 747. He will give an account to the Lord for the decisions made in his home, and he forgets it or rejects it at his own peril.

NOTES

Chapter 1

1. Cited by Ben Patterson, *Waiting* (Downers Grove, Ill.: InterVarsity Press, 1989), p. 41.

2. James C. Dobson, *Straight Talk to Men and Their Wives* (Waco, Tex.: Word, Inc., 1980), p. 21.

3. Statistics from Hans Finzel, *Help! I'm a Baby-Boomer* (Wheaton, Ill.: Victor, 1989), pp. 85-87; Joe White, *Orphans at Home* (Phoenix: Questar, 1988), p. 43; and *Kids In Crisis* newsletter, PO Box 3512, Irving, Texas 75015.

4. Dave Johnson, *The Light Behind the Star* (Sisters, Ore.: Questar, 1989), p. 13. Used by permission.

5. White, p. 44.

6. Tom Peters and Nancy Austin, *A Passion for Excellence* (New York: Random House, 1985), p. 496.

7. J. Robert Clinton, *The Making of a Leader* (Colorado Springs: NavPress, 1988), p. 203.

Chapter 2

1. William Raspberry, "Save the Boys," *The Washington Post*, 18 July 1989.

2. Charles Colson, *Against the Night* (Ann Arbor, Mich.: Servant, 1989), p. 73ff.

3. Don Lewis, transcript of testimony before the Select Committee on Children, Youth and Families, U. S. House of Representatives, 25 July 1989.

4. Richard John Neuhaus, cited by Raspberry, ibid.

5. Phon Hudkins, cited by Raspberry, ibid.

6. Dave Simmons, unpublished notes, "Dad, The Family Shepherd," P.O. Box 21445, Little Rock, Arkansas 72221.

7. Stephen Clark, *Man and Woman In Christ* (Ann Arbor, Mich.: Servant, 1980), p. 64.

8. *World Book Encyclopedia*, 1959, s.v. "Industrial Revolution," vol. 9, p. 3752.

9. *World Book Encyclopedia*, 1959, s.v. "Colonial Life in America," vol. 3, p. 1576.

10. Ibid., p. 1570.

11. *World Book Encyclopedia*, 1959, s.v. "Industrial Revolution," vol. 9, p. 3753.

12. Weldon Hardenbrook, *Missing From Action*

(Nashville: Thomas Nelson, 1987), p. 11.

13. Samuel Osherson, *Finding Our Fathers* (New York: Fawcett/Columbine, 1986), p. 6.

14. Tim Kimmel, *Legacy of Love* (Portland, Ore.: Multnomah Press, 1989), p. 35. Kimmel has an excellent resource here called "A Checklist for My Child's Future." Highly recommended.

15. Cited by Patrick Morley, *The Man in the Mirror* (Nashville: Wolgemuth & Hyatt, 1989), p. 95.

16. James Carrol, cited by Osherson, p. 30.

17. Osherson, p. 6.

18. Ibid., p. 54.

19. Ibid., p. 7.

20. Cited by William Peterson, *Martin Luther Had a Wife* (Wheaton, Ill.: Tyndale House, 1983), p. 75.

Chapter 3

1. Richard Saul Wurman, *Information Anxiety* (New York: Doubleday, 1988), p. 109.

2. Dennis Rainey, *Family Life Conference Notebook* (unpublished), p. 22.

3. Warren Wiersbe, *The Integrity Crisis* (Nashville: Oliver Nelson, 1988) p. 40.

4. Alexis de Tocqueville, cited by *Disciplemaker* newsletter, October 1989.

5. Randy Alcorn, "Strategies to Keep from Falling," *Leadership* (Winter 1988), p. 44.

6. Alcorn, p. 45.

7. Donald McCullough, *Waking from the American Dream* (Downers Grove, Ill.: InterVarsity, 1988), p. 87.

8. Donald Joy, *Unfinished Business* (Wheaton, Ill.: Victor Books, 1989), p. 159.

9. Robert Farrar Capon, cited by McCullough, p. 117.

10. Charles Swindoll, *Rise & Shine* (Portland, Ore.: Multnomah Press, 1989), p. 198.

11. John Walvoord, *Bible Knowledge Commentary* (Wheaton, Ill.: Victor Books, 1985), p. 468.

12. Charles Haddon Spurgeon, *Lectures to My Students* (Grand Rapids: Zondervan, 1954), p. 13.

13. Robert Murray McCheyne, cited by Spurgeon, p. 8.

14. Wurman, p. 15.

Chapter 4

1. "I Only Have Eyes for You," (Harry Warren, Al Dubin). © 1934 Warner Bros. Inc. (Renewed). All rights reserved. Used by permission.

2. Bill Hull, *The Disciple Making Pastor* (Old Tappan, N. J.: Fleming H. Revell, 1988), p. 62.

Chapter 5

1. George Gallup, cited in *Leadership*, Fall 1987, pp. 15, 19.

2. Raymond E. Vath, M.D., *Counseling Those with Eating Disorders* (Waco, Tex.: Word, 1986), p. 36.

3. Derek Kidner, *Psalms 1-72* (Downers Grove, Ill.: InterVarsity, 1973), p. 48.

4. John Piper, *Desiring God* (Portland, Ore.: Multnomah Press, 1986), pp. 127-129.

5. James Underwood Crockett, *Trees* (New York: Time Life Books, 1972), p. 16.

Chapter 6

1. Dr. Kenneth Cooper, *Aerobics* (New York: Bantam, 1968), p. 13.

2. E. M. Bounds, *Power Through Prayer* (Grand Rapids: Baker, 1965), p. 46.

3. Colson, p. 165.

4. D. Martyn Lloyd-Jones, *The Christian in Warfare* (Grand Rapids: Baker, 1976), p. 153.

5. Piper, p. 182.

6. Swindoll, p. 211.

Chapter 7

1. Excerpted with permission from "Miracle in the Blizzard," by Henry Hurt, *Reader's Digest*, February 1990. © 1990 by the Reader's Digest Assn., Inc., p. 105.

2. Ibid., p. 104.

3. Ibid., p. 105.

4. Ibid., p. 108.

5. Fritz Reinecker, *A Linguistic Key to the Greek New Testament* (Grand Rapids: Zondervan, 1980).

6. Piper, p. 182.

7. John Gardner, *On Leadership* (New York: Free Press, 1990), p. 33.

8. Warren Bennis, *On Becoming a Leader* (New York: Addison-Wesley, 1989), p. 196.

9. *Marriage Partnership*, Winter 1990.

10. Carl D. Windsor, *On This Day* (Nashville: Thomas Nelson, 1989), p. 53.

11. Rienecker, p. 757.

12. Clifton Fadiman, *The Little, Brown Book of Anecdotes* (Boston: Little, Brown, 1985), p. 160.

13. I am indebted to Michelle Coffman for this definition.

14. Ted W. Engstrom, *The Fine Art of Mentoring* (Nashville: Wolgemuth & Hyatt, 1989), p. 33.

15. Bennis, p. 195.

16. Gardner, p. 107.

Chapter 8

1. Barbara Kantrowitz, "Three's a Crowd," *Newsweek*, 1 September 1986, p. 68.

2. Ibid., p. 69.

3. Ibid., p. 70.

4. Ibid.

Chapter 9

1. John Piper, *What's the Difference?* (Wheaton, Ill.: The Council on Biblical Manhood and Womanhood, 1989), p. 9.

2. Peter Wyden, *Growing Up Straight* (New York: Stein & Day, 1968).

3. Hardenbrook, p. 23.

4. George Gilder, *Men and Marriage* (Gretna, La.: Pelican, 1986), p. XI.

5. Sueann Robinson Ambrom and Neil J. Salkind, *Child Development* (New York: Holt, Rinehart & Winston, 1984).

6. Gary Bauer, Family Research Council Newsletter, December 1989, p. 1.

7. Reinecker, p. 540.

8. Ibid., p. 582.

9. William Hendriksen, *New Testament Commentary: Ephesians* (Grand Rapids: Baker, 1967), p. 261.

10. Clark, p. 395.

11. Robert Coles, cited in "Reflections," *Christianity Today*, 16 June 1989 p. 45.

12. Kay Marshall Strom, *In the Name of Submission* (Portland, Ore.: Multnomah Press, 1986), p. 63.

13. Reinecker, p. 540.

14. Dr. Peter Blitchington, *Sex Roles and the Christian Family* (Wheaton, Ill.: Tyndale House, 1984), p. 121.

15. Charles R. Swindoll, *Chuck Swindoll Talks about Fatherhood* (Pomona, Calif.: Focus on the Family, 1989), p. 9.

16. Hendriksen, p. 62.

17. Ibid., p. 262.

18. Kenneth Taylor, cited by Lloyd Cory, *Quotable Quotations* (Wheaton, Ill.: Victor, 1985).

19. Dave Simmons, unpublished notes, "Dad, the Family Shepherd."

20. Blitchington, p. 108.

Chapter 10

1. George Grant, *Grand Illusions: The Legacy of Planned Parenthood*, cited by Beverly LaHaye, "Victimizing Our Children," *Concerned Women of America*, November 1988, p. 19.

2. Tom Minnery, "Why Gays Want Marriage," *Citizen*, July 1989, p. 3.

3. Josh McDowell, *How to Help Your Child Say No to Sexual Pressure* (Waco, Tex.: Word, Inc., 1987), p. 101.

4. Connie Marshner, *Decent Exposure: How to Teach Your Kids About Sex* (Nashville: Wolgemuth & Hyatt, 1988), p. 179.

5. Gardner, p. 51.

6. McDowell, p. 99.

7. Ibid., p. 44.

Chapter 11

1. Finzel, p. 9.

2. Jane Bryant Quinn, "Laying Bets on the '90s," *Newsweek*, 15 January 1990, p. 53.

3. Judith Wallerstein, *Second Chances* (New York: Ticknor & Fields, 1989), p. 308.

Appendix

1. Dave Roper, "Helping a Hurting Marriage," *Discovery Papers* (7 July 1974), p. 1.

2. Dr. Wayne House, "Caught in the Middle," *Kindred Spirit*, Summer 1989, p. 12.

3. Piper, *Desiring God*, p. 179.

4. James B. Hurley, *Man and Woman in Biblical Perspective* (Grand Rapids: Zondervan, 1981), p. 126.

5. Cited by Clark, p. 145.

Study/Discussion
Guide

CHAPTER ONE

Point Man
on Patrol

Taking Aim at These Issues

1. GETTING A GRIP ON THE ENEMY'S STRATEGY. Reread pages 14 through 16 in *Point Man,* then talk about these questions with the guys in your group.

    a. If you were the Vietcong watching a group of GIs approach, what would be your strategy for defeating the American patrol? What weapons would you use to do that?

    b. Now switch gears for a second. You're still in a war, but it's the 1990s and you're in a moral jungle with *Satan* waiting to ambush you. This chapter talks about two strategies he uses to do that. The first is to *effectively alienate and sever the relationship you have with your wife.*

If you were advising Satan about weapons he could use to destroy your relationship with your wife, what would you tell him?

c. The second strategy he uses is to *effectively alienate and sever your relationship with your children.*

Again, if you were advising Satan about how he could best attack *you* in this area, what would you tell him?

2. THE SAD STATE OF THE AMERICAN FAMILY. Reread the statistics on pages 17 and 18 that outline what's going on in the American family today. Discuss these questions with one another.

a. One of the hardest things for men to come to grips with is, "These things *could happen to me and my family.*" Why is that so tough to admit?

b. Read 1 Corinthians 10:1-13. Read all thirteen verses to get the context, but set your sights specifically on verse 13. The lesson for us there is that *just because we're Christians doesn't mean we won't turn our backs on God and our families.* In fact, verse 12 implies that the guy who thinks he can't fall is the one who probably will! (See Proverbs 11:2, 16:18, and 29:23 if you need some backup on this.)

So, the question is, Why *won't* one or more of the things listed on pages 17 and 18 happen to you and your family? In other words, what are you doing to *actively prevent* them from happening?

c. Some of you may have already been a victim of Satan's attacks. Share with the other guys things you've learned that can keep *them* off the casualty list.

3. HAVING THE BEST OF BOTH WORLDS. Reread the paragraph about Tom Peters on page 26. He talks there about a struggle we all face—the desire to have a full, satisfying personal life and a full, satisfying, hard-working professional life. But, as Peters points out, we can't have both. Discuss these questions with the group.

a. Have you come to grips with the reality that you *can't* have both?

b. What factors from *your past* make this easy or difficult to accept?

c. What factors in your *present experience* make it easy or difficult to accept?

4. GETTING READY FOR SATAN'S ATTACK. There's no doubt we're in a war for our families, and Satan is taking aim at us. When a man gets serious about leading his family for Christ, he can, in the words of this chapter, ". . . expect the shelling to start." And, like a mobile SCUD missile, he can launch an attack anytime, anywhere, anyplace—and at *anything* in our lives he wants to.

a. In what ways is Satan lobbing his SCUDs into your life? Are there any areas where you feel like your defenses are starting to crack? If so, ask the guys in the group to pray for you.

b. If a man is passive and indifferent to the things of God and the spiritual leadership of his home, attack is not necessary. He is already "neutralized" (p. 28). If you're not being attacked, how has Satan already neutralized you? What is it going to take to get you back in the fight?

CHAPTER TWO

Save the Boys

Taking Aim at These Issues

1. HOMES WHERE DAD WASN'T AROUND. Many of us came from families where, unfortunately, our dads weren't around much—or if they were, it either didn't make much difference or we wished they *weren't* there. If you came from a home like that, discuss these questions with the group.

(Special note: Some of the guys in your group have come from bad homes, others from good ones. So, leave time to discuss these questions and the ones in question 2, below.)

    a. How did your dad's lack of ability to be a good father make you feel when you were growing

up? How does it make you feel now that you're
an adult?

b. What are some things your dad did that have
had a negative influence on your life? How do
you know you won't repeat the same mistakes
with *your* kids?

c. If you're still harboring resentment or anger
toward your dad, how does that affect you
each day? Have you ever forgiven him for the
things he did wrong?

d. What was your dad's relationship like with *his*
dad? What kind of clues does that give you
about what your dad went through and the
hurt he's endured?

e. Name at least one *positive* thing you learned
from your dad.

2. HOMES WHERE DAD WAS AROUND. There are also those
of us who grew up in a home where our dads were a
positive influence in our lives. If that describes you, talk
with the guys in your group about these questions:

a. What were some of the things your dad did
that meant a lot to you when you were a boy?

b. What values did your dad try to teach you?
What were some of the most effective ways he
did that?

c. What things did your dad do for you growing
up that you want to pass on to your wife and
children?

d. What did you most admire about your father?
What will you most remember about him after
he dies?

3. WHAT WE WANT OUR KIDS TO LEARN FROM US. One of the primary principles of fathering this chapter talks about is *less time = less influence*. Read the bottom of page 40 through page 41. Now, take a few minutes and use the space below to write out the important habits and character traits you want your children to learn from watching you.

The habits and character traits I want to model and teach my kids are: (If you need some ideas, read Deuteronomy 6:4-9, Psalm 147:10-11; Proverbs 1:8-9; Jeremiah 9:23-24; Micah 6:8; and Ephesians 6:4. You can also take a look at the list on page 42.)

1. _____

2. _____

3. _____

(Use another sheet of paper if you have other ideas or thoughts).

Share your answers with the group. Tell them *why* you wrote down what you did.

4. BEING A GOOD DAD MEANS "BEING THERE" PHYSICALLY. It's important to remember that when it comes to being a godly dad, error increases with distance. "In other words, if I am going to be the family leader that God has called me to be, then I must BE THERE. On site. Consistently" (p. 43). Keeping that in mind, talk about these questions.

    a. If most of us were honest, we'd admit that, at times, we don't feel like being around our kids. Why?

    b. What are some of the challenges you face in trying to be with your kids consistently?

    c. Share some ideas with one another about ways

you can overcome the things that keep you from spending quantity time with your children. Use the space below to jot down ideas you like.

_____

_____

_____

_____

5. BEING A GOOD DAD ALSO MEANS "BEING THERE" EMOTIONALLY. "The interviews that I have had with men in their thirties and forties convince me that the psychological or physical absence of father from their families is one of the great underestimated tragedies of our times" (p. 45).

    a. Do you find being close to your children *emotionally* easy or hard to do? Why? (Remember, a lot of this may have to do with experiences you had with *your* dad.)

    b. What are some things you could do that would make you better at filling your kids' emotional tanks?

6. BELIEVING YOU CAN REALLY MAKE A DIFFERENCE. Reread page 47 through the paragraph on page 49 that ends, ". . . It will be the greatest and most fulfilling task of your life." Then, talk about these questions.

    a. Most of us, if we're honest, *want* to believe that one man can make a difference, but we sometimes have a hard time really believing it. What are some of the things that keep you from accepting this fact?

    (Hopefully, your discussion about this question will help convince you that you really *can* make a difference. If you need a little more convincing, read Exodus 4:1-17, Psalm 1, Luke 7:24-28, and Philippians 4:13.)

b. Use the space below to write out a commitment to your children to be a godly father. Express it in your own words. Do it *before* you leave this session. Then, share it with your wife and kids.

(For extra credit, have it framed and place it in your house as a sign of your commitment to them. Seeing it in the hallway each day will keep you honest!)

MY PLEDGE OF LOVE AND COMMITMENT TO EACH OF YOU:

_____

_____

_____

_____

_____

_____

_____

_____

_____

_____

_____

_____

_____

_____

_____

_____

Chapter Three

Real Men Don't

Taking Aim at These Issues

1. Why We Fall Prey to Adultery. This chapter defines an affair as "an escape from reality, or a search for meaning outside the marriage" (p. 56). Think about that definition for a moment and then discuss this question.

> Think about someone you know who has been involved in adultery. Does the above statement capture their motivation? If so, why was that such a driving force behind their involvement?

2. Finishing Well. ". . . In this war, Christian men of all vocations are going down. *Men who started well*, men who were at one time committed to Jesus Christ and their families, walked into an ambush and so destroyed their credibility and integrity" (p. 57). Keeping that thought in mind, discuss this question.

> Why is it so *easy* to start well and so *hard* to finish well?

3. ADMITTING WE COULD BE "HOOKED" EMOTIONALLY. One of the hardest things for a man to admit is that another woman might be able to sink "an emotional hook" in his jaw. Randy Alcorn suggests there are three questions we need to ask ourselves to see if we're on the verge of adultery (p. 60).

> a. Do I look forward in a special way to my appointments with this person?
>
> b. Do I seek to meet with her away from the office in a more casual environment?
>
> c. Do I prefer that my co-workers not know I'm meeting with her again?

Discuss these questions:

a. What does 1 Corinthians 6:18-20 tell us to do in the face of temptation?

b. Why does Paul say we should flee?

c. Brainstorm some ideas with the group about specific, practical ways to flee. Examples: ask for a different work partner, pray for the woman you're attracted to, etc. Use the space below to record those ideas.

_____

_____

_____

_____

4. *ADMITTING IT COULD HAPPEN TO US.* "Have you ever noticed how many men in the Bible failed in the second half of life? Our enemy is so cunning that he will wait forty or even fifty years to set a trap. . . . That's why we can never deceive ourselves into thinking we are somehow 'above' sexual sin. The moment you [do] you can be sure that your carcass will one day be hanging in cold storage" (p. 66). Each guy answer these two questions.

  a. Do I believe *I* could commit adultery? Why or why not?

  b. What am I actively doing right now to make sure I never do?

5. *THINKING THE GRASS WOULD BE GREENER.* Pages 66 and 67 talk about the fact that when a man leaves his wife for another woman, he takes his biggest problem with him—*himself.* Toss this question around for a minute.

If a guy thinks it could be better with someone else, what crucial mistake is he making?

6. *COUNTING THE COST OF ADULTERY.* "*In the New Testament, forgiveness is free but leadership is earned.* It is earned by the power of a man's life. Sin, though forgiven, always sets off practical consequences" (p. 74). Look at 2 Samuel 12:7-15 and then peruse chapters 12 through 18. David knew the practical effects of sin—he experienced them the rest of his life. Talk about this question with each other.

What are some of the consequences you've seen others endure for their adultery? Is it worth the price they've paid?

CHAPTER FOUR

One-Woman Kind of Man

Taking Aim at These Issues

1. CONVENIENT COMMITMENT. "The spirit of our age, whether expressed in athletics, business, politics, or marriage, maintains that commitments should be honored only while convenient. When a commitment becomes inconvenient, bag it. . . . Generally speaking, our society believes that only one commitment sounds good: The right to be happy" (p. 84). Discuss these questions with one another.

    a. In what ways do you see this attitude expressed in your world (i.e., at work, friendships, family, etc.)?

    b. In what areas of your life do you believe you have the *right* to be happy?

    c. Do you agree or disagree with the following statement? True happiness is the result of responsible living.

    d. In what areas of your life do you have the right to be responsible?

2. BEING MEN WHO ARE ALWAYS FAITHFUL. *Semper Fidelis* is the motto of the Marine Corps. It means "always faithful." Regardless of the cost or the convenience. It means in the 100-yard dash of marriage we don't run the fifty-, sixty-, or ninety-five-yard dash. It means we suck it up and finish—and finish well. Page 88 suggests two bottom-line commitments all of us need to make in order to do just that. They are: adopt *Semper Fidelis* as our personal motto, and "burn our ships" by becoming a one-woman kind of man.

    a. Why is *Semper Fidelis* so important to the Marine Corps?

    b. Why is *Semper Fidelis* so important to your family?

What does it mean to be a one-woman man? First, it means we should be . . .

3. A ONE-WOMAN MAN WITH OUR EYES. That doesn't mean we don't notice beautiful women, but it does mean we know the difference between looking and looking with lust. It also means we have a *predetermined plan* for avoiding lust.

    a. What are some of the differences between looking and looking with lust?

    b. What kind of predetermined plan will keep *you* from being picked off by Satan in a weak moment? (Have each guy share the practical steps he thinks he needs to take. Use the space

below to jot down ideas you like. You may
want to reread pages 94 through 97 for some
initial ideas to get you started.)

_____

_____

_____

We should also be . . .

4. A ONE-WOMAN MAN WITH OUR MIND. "Temptation itself
is not a sin, but a call to battle. . . . *You cannot prevent
wrong thoughts from coming into your mind.* That's
temptation. It is not wrong to be tempted. . . . But
what you do with that thought in the next microsecond will determine whether that thought will turn
into sin" (pp. 98-99). But for a lot of us, learning to
seize that thought for Christ is like learning how to
dribble left-handed.

  a. What are some struggles you've faced in con-
     trolling your thought life?

  b. Can you trace those struggles to a particular
     event or time in your life when they became a
     problem? If so, what triggered it?

  c. This chapter talks about being a "Dick Butkus"
     when it comes to our thought lives. "When that
     wrong thought enters your mind, you hit it like
     Butkus. You capture, seize, gouge, and strangle
     it to the obedience of Christ." What are some
     ways you can ask the Holy Spirit to help you
     become aggressive with your thought life? (See
     page 104 for an idea to get you started.) Use
     the following spaces for notes.

_____

_____

_____

_____

We must also be . . .

5. A ONE-WOMAN MAN WITH OUR LIPS: Being a one-woman man means we are faithful with our lips. We shouldn't flirt or make jokes. In the words of this chapter, "Marriage is sacred. Marriage is holy. It's nothing to kid around about" (p. 105).

> What are some of the common ways we tend to be unfaithful to our wives with our lips? How can we avoid those mistakes in the future?

There are two more keys to being a one-woman man. The first is we must be . . .

6. A ONE-WOMAN MAN WITH OUR HANDS. "A one-woman man is careful about the way he touches the opposite sex" (p. 105).

> a. What are some of the ways we can touch women in an unhealthy way and get away with it?
>
> b. What are the standards you think *you* ought to have in order to keep from touching other women inappropriately? (Each guy should answer this.)

Finally, we should be . . .

7. A ONE-WOMAN MAN WITH OUR FEET. "First Corinthians 6:18 says it flat out: 'Flee from sexual immorality.' That's how a one-woman man deals with movies, magazines, videos, or any kind of situation that is counterproductive to marriage commitment. He flees" (p. 106).

> On page 106, several things are listed that describe what it means to flee immorality (i.e., not reading a pornographic magazine for its artistic value;

walking out of a movie, if need be; etc.). What other things can you add to the list? Use the space below to record the good ideas you hear. (Refer to question 4 under chapter 3 for other ideas.)

_____

_____

_____

_____

_____

_____

_____

_____

_____

_____

CHAPTER FIVE

Anorexic Men and Their Bulimic Cousins

Taking Aim at These Issues

1. ADMITTING THAT, A LOT OF TIMES, WE DON'T WANT TO READ OUR BIBLES. "Thousands of Christian men have spiritual anorexia, and that is why they are ineffective in leading their families. What is spiritual anorexia? *Spiritual anorexia is an aversion to reading the Scripture."* (p. 113). Talk about these questions with your group.

 a. Deuteronomy 32:46-47 says, "Take to your heart all the words with which I am warning you today, which you shall command your sons to observe carefully, even all the words of this law. For it is not an idle word for you; indeed, *it is your life."* If that's true, then why don't we read our Bibles more than we do?

b. On a scale of one to ten, one being "very little desire" and ten being "a great deal of desire," where, *honestly*, would you rate yourself in your desire to study and know God's Word? Mark your answer below.

1	2	3	4	5	6	7	8	9	1 0

very little desire   great
                                                       desire

Now, talk about these things with your group.

- If you rated yourself on the low end of the scale, share why you feel that way. What would it take to move you closer to a ten?

- If you rated yourself on the higher end of the scale, share any experiences you've had that have increased your desire to learn from His Word.

2. READING THE BIBLE IS A DAILY DECISION. Reread the bottom of page 115 and all of page 116. We can be strong in our commitment to read God's Word and have been at it a long time, but each of us still fights the temptation to skip it. Discuss these questions with one another.

a. What activities (like reading the paper) tempt you away from spending time in God's Word?

b. What helps you overcome that temptation and stay on course?

c. What practical advice can you offer one another that will help you be more consistent?

3. GOD'S WORD GIVES US THE PERSPECTIVE WE NEED. This chapter gives us three important things God's Word does in our lives (p. 117). It . . .

- reminds us there is a God who rules the affairs of our lives.

- reminds us of what is true.

- reinforces our convictions.

Take a moment, look at this list, and then discuss these questions.

   a. Of these three, which do you need to be reminded of the most? Why?

   b. In which of these areas do you most often have a head-on collision with the world? Why?

   c. Which of these give you the greatest comfort, encouragement, and stability during tough times?

4. REALIZING WE DON'T WANT TO APPLY SCRIPTURE TO OUR LIVES. "Spiritually speaking, bulimia is the inconsistent reading or hearing of the Word without personal application (p. 119). Being hearers and doers of the Word means our ". . . goal is to go from [spiritual] ignorance to knowledge to obedience" (p. 121). Discuss these questions.

   a. What's the biggest challenge you face in applying scriptural truth more consistently?

   b. Ignorance to knowledge to obedience is the applicational process we must go through with Scripture. Which of those steps is hardest for you? Why?

   c. Think about some of the successes you've had in applying scriptural truth. What did you learn from those experiences that can help you now?

   d. Think about some of the failures you've had in

applying Scripture. Again, what did you learn that can help you be more consistent?

5. MEDITATION IS THE KEY TO ANOREXIA AND BULIMIA. "The righteous man is not anorexic. He delights in getting clear direction form the Word of God, and this divine direction gives him satisfaction. . . . Meditation is to the soul what digestion is to the body. That is, meditation is spiritual digestion" (p. 122).

What are some of the differences between reading Scripture and *meditating* on it? (See page 123 for ideas to prod your thinking). Why is that difference so important to our spiritual health?

6. IF WE ARE ANOREXIC OR BULIMIC, WE DON'T HAVE TO LOSE HEART. The key is to become a spiritual self starter. Here are some ways to do that.

- Read through the Bible in one year.
- Listen to the Bible during your commute or workout times.
- Memorize Scripture.
- Get involved in a Bible study fellowship.
- Form a small accountability group.

Circle two things from the above list you want to commit to that will help you be a more consistent, faithful man of God's Word. (If the group can think of others, add them to the list.) Share with the group the two you've chosen. *The group should make a commitment to "check in" with one another over the next few weeks to make sure everyone's being faithful to their commitment.*

7. WHAT IT TAKES TO BE AN OAK OF RIGHTEOUSNESS. "A fully developed oak tree is a magnificent specimen of God's creation. We are impressed with its commanding and imposing presence. That describes precisely the man who has his roots sunk deep into the truth of God's Word" (p. 127).

    a. Reread pages 128 (beginning with, "When my dad was in his early forties . . .") through the paragraph on page 131 that ends, "But there are no guarantees." Have you ever known someone like Steve's dad? If so, describe the kind of impact he had on your life.

    b. "Anne Morrow Lindbergh once said, 'Only when a tree has fallen can you take the measure of it. It is the same with a man.'" (p. 131). Discuss why that is true.

    c. Here's a challenge for you. If you want to leave the same kind of legacy for your children that Steve's dad did for him, sign the following commitment sheet and have someone in the group act as a witness.

Before God, my family, and the guys in my group, I want to make a rock-solid commitment to being a man of God's Word for the rest of my life.

    In order to do that, I will

_____

_____

_____

_____

Signed _____

Witnessed by _____

Date _____

CHAPTER SIX

Aerobic Kneeling

Taking Aim at These Issues

1. REALIZING WE MUST TRAIN FOR THE MARATHON OF THE CHRISTIAN LIFE. "Endurance is needed to run the race of the Christian life. You don't need endurance to run one hundred yards. You do, however, need endurance to run 26 miles, 385 yards. . . . That's why there are no starting blocks in the Christian life. . . . When you're running a marathon, your focus isn't on your start—it's on your finish" (p. 135). The key to how any of us finishes is *how well we've trained*. Toss this question around with one another for a moment.

> How do you stay in shape spiritually? Is what you're doing enough to keep you in the marathon?

2. PRAYER IS THE BEST AEROBIC EXERCISE THERE IS. "A spiritual self starter is a man who is in good spiritual shape. That means he does two things: 1) He consistently eats the nutritious diet of Scripture and 2) he consistently spends time in aerobic kneeling. *Prayer is the exercise of the man who is a spiritual self-starter.* . . . A marathon runner not only trains efficiently but eats correctly. Both enable him to have physical endurance. The same is true of the Christian life" (p. 137). Discuss these questions.

> a. Prayer gives us the opportunity to walk into the office of the CEO of the universe and talk with him about anything we want, for as long as we want, anytime we want. (What executive or politician in the country wouldn't want the same privilege with his superior?) If that's the privilege prayer gives us, why don't we take advantage of it more often?
>
> b. This chapter suggests that thirty minutes, three times a week is a good goal to shoot for with our prayer life. What's keeping you from doing that right now? What would it take to get those things out of the way? Why not get them out of the way right now?
>
> c. As you examine your life, are there any things you've made more of a priority than your prayer life? Why?
>
> d. What do you think would happen if thousands of Christian men got their priorities right and started to get serious about prayer?

3. THINKING ABOUT WHAT WE SHOULD PRAY FOR. "If we're going to be spiritual leaders for our wives and children . . . we need to make time to soak ourselves in God's

Word; we need time to chew on what the Scripture is saying to us; we need time to come before God and ask Him to give us the wisdom we need to be His men in this world" (p. 145). Talk about these things for a few minutes.

    a. In what areas of your life do you most need God's wisdom? Why? Have you asked Him for it?

    b. If you came up with a list of things you most wanted to talk with God about, what would be on it? (For some great ideas, reread the paragraph on page 145 that begins, "We need to come before Him. . . .")

    c. Now take an honest look at the things on your list. How many of them reflect your priorities? How many reflect God's?

    d. How do the things you've discovered in the above passage change your perspective on your prayers?

4. COMING UP WITH A PLAN FOR AEROBIC SPIRITUAL FITNESS. This chapter suggests five things for coming up with a plan.

- Plan a time.
- Plan a place.
- Make a list.
- Begin with Scripture.
- Make yourself accountable.

If you need more information on these, reread pages 148 to 152. Now, discuss these questions.

    a. As you look at this list, what's the hardest thing for you to do? Why?

    b. Take each item on the list and briefly tell the

other guys in the group what an ideal plan would be for you with each area. For instance, "The best time for me is. . . ."

5. DEALING WITH THE HIGH HURDLES OF AEROBIC KNEELING.
"Aerobic kneeling comes under the category of spiritual discipline. It takes time to develop any kind of discipline. As you attempt to pray, you will encounter boredom, frustration, and monotony. As you attempt to develop these disciplines, you will encounter resistance" (p. 152). Talk about these questions together.

    a. Have you ever been successful developing a new habit? What kind of qualities and talents did it take to be successful? How could you use those things to be successful in your prayer life?

    b. Look at the list on page 152 of some of the common hurdles we can run into when we're praying. Can you relate to any of them? Which ones? Why? What others would you add to the list?

    c. Brainstorm with one another about ways to effectively get over these hurdles. Use the space on this page to jot down ideas you like.

_____

_____

_____

_____

_____

_____

_____

_____

Husband and Wife Teamwork in the Marriage Cockpit

Taking Aim at These Issues

1. GETTING A GRIP ON THE MONTANA-RICE PRINCIPLE. "Joe Montana and Jerry Rice are one of the most dangerous passing combinations in the history of the National Football League. To watch Montana and Rice operate is sheer bliss" (p. 163).

    a. Think about some other great combinations and examples of teamwork in sports. What are some of the principles that make these guys/teams so good?

    b. "Trust is what motivates people to follow our leadership, whether at work or home. And trust must be earned . . ." (p. 165). What are some of the things you do that make it difficult for your wife to trust you and thus submit to your leadership?

2. KNOWING THE DIFFERENCE BETWEEN BIBLICAL LEADERSHIP AND AUTHORITARIANISM. On page 168 there's a list of things that characterize someone who's being an authoritarian. Reread that list then discuss these questions.

    a. Have you ever been around someone who exhibited some or all of these characteristics? What was that experience like? What did you learn about authority from that person?

    b. Be honest. Do you exhibit any of these on a consistent basis with *your* family? If so, why? In other words, what attitudes and experiences have led you to be an authoritarian with them?

    c. If you tend to be authoritarian, how do you think it affects your wife and kids?

    Going The Extra Mile At Home: Ask your wife and children how it affects them.

In the following three questions, we'll deal with what it means for a husband to be a mature leader. First, being a mature leader means

3. LOVING YOUR WIFE SACRIFICIALLY. "For some reason, wives have an uncanny ability to measure our sacrificial love with the accuracy of a yardstick. . . . They intuitively know there is a direct correlation between service and sacrifice. And it usually comes out in the little things that spring from a right attitude" (pp. 169-170).

    a. Read Ephesians 5:25-31. What are some characteristics of sacrificial love this passage talks about? (For another passage that talks about sacrifice, see Philippians 2:1-8.) How can these characteristics express themselves in *everyday acts of sacrifice* for your wife? Use the space below to jot down ideas you hear.

_____

_____

_____

_____

b. It's often true that actions follow attitudes. What are some *attitudes* we can fall prey to that affect our ability to love our wives sacrificially?

c. What are some creative ways you can use your wife's barometer for sacrifice to help you be a more mature leader? Take notes on this one!

_____

_____

_____

_____

Second, being a mature leader means . . .

4. LOVING YOUR WIFE WITH UNDERSTANDING. First Peter 3:7 talks about living with our wives in "an understanding way." "The word *understanding* carries with it the idea of insight and tactfulness. . . . What is difficult for any wife, regardless of whom she is married to, is to be misunderstood" (p. 171).

a. What are some common ways we misunderstand our wives?

b. Brainstorm for a moment and come up with

some practical ways to *avoid* misunderstanding our wives. Use the space below to record the group's suggestions.

_____

_____

_____

c. Now think of some creative things you can do to *communicate* understanding to your wife. Again, use the space below for ideas you want to remember.

_____

_____

_____

Finally, being a mature leader means . . .

5. *LOVING YOUR WIFE WITH VERBAL PRAISE.* "Verbal praise is a rare commodity in our world. That's why Mark Twain said he could live for sixty days off one compliment. . . . There are severe consequences for the man who refuses to correct his errors with his wife. If you do not . . . let her know she is valuable to you, your prayers will be hindered" (p. 172). Toss these questions around.

a. You may deeply appreciate your wife in your heart, but when was the last time you verbally expressed your appreciation to her?

b. Think of a time when you received a compliment or pat on the back that meant a lot to you. How did that make you feel? What did it do for your motivation? For your self image?

c. What things make it difficult for you to love your wife with verbal praise? (If you're experiencing some unresolved tension or crisis with your wife, ask the guys in your group for their prayers and insight on how to resolve the problem.)

6. *THE VALUE OF MUTUAL ACCOUNTABILITY.* "The vast majority of men have wives who want their husbands to win. . . . Gentlemen, your wife is a strategic gift to you! She has eyes that see what you don't, a mind that assimilates information from a different perspective, a heart with sensitivities you do not possess, and a personality with strengths that offset your weaknesses. . . . That's why you must tap into her perspective as you lead your family" (p. 174). Discuss these things with the group.

a. Everyone name at least one strength, quality, or gift your wife has that you don't have. How has God used that to make your relationship better? *By the way: tell your wife what you've said. It will make her day!*

b. Most of us don't think of our wives in the terms described above. What are some of the most common ways we're tempted to view them? Now read these passages together: Proverbs 18:22 and 31:10-12. What are some of the things these verses tell us about God's perspective on our wives?

c. Most of us would also have to admit that, at times, we have a hard time putting a lot of stock in what our wives think. Why? How do you think that makes them feel? Talk about practical steps you can take to avoid that in the future. (Use the space below for ideas you want to try.)

_____

_____

d. On a scale of one to ten, one being "not hard" and ten being "very hard," how difficult is it for you to be accountable to your wife?

_____

1	2	3	4	5	6	7	8	9	10
not hard									very hard

Share with the other guys what you put *and why*.

7. THE INTIMIDATION FACTOR. "One way that some men keep from being mutually accountable is through intimidation. . . . A 'high control' husband can easily . . . run his home the way he wants, and he doesn't want suggestions from anyone—especially his wife. After all, he may think, it's her 'job' to submit to his authority" (pp. 176, 178). Talk together about these questions.

a. Have you ever tried to intimidate your wife into submission? How did it go?

b. Have you ever tried to intimidate her so that she wouldn't contradict or challenge your opinion? How did that go?

c. In what ways can using intimidation backfire on you?

8. UNDERSTANDING WHAT MUTUAL SUBMISSION REALLY MEANS. "Let me be clear. Mutual submission does not mean that the husband and wife take turns being the head of the home. . . . It means, gentlemen, that you take the lead in your submission to Christ to such an extent that you become a model for your wife. . . . I have yet to meet a Christian woman whose husband provides this kind of leadership who has difficulty with the idea of biblical submission" (pp. 181-182).

   a. Are there any authority figures in your life you're having a difficult time submitting to right now? Why? If your wife sees you "bucking" that person's authority, what kind of effect might that have on her willingness to submit to you?

   b. Most of us would admit that one of our greatest fears about submitting to each other is that it may mean we'll be treated unfairly or taken advantage of. What does 1 Peter 2:18-24 say about all of that? What did Christ rely on that allowed him to submit when He knew he would be abused? How can that help us as we submit to the authorities in our lives?

CHAPTER EIGHT

The Birth of
a Tangent

Taking Aim at These Issues

1. THERE ARE TWO KINDS OF CHILDLESS COUPLES IN THE WORLD.

    a. The first type of couple would love to have children but can't. Why are these couples willing to make such extraordinary personal sacrifices in order to have children?

    b. The second type of couple is able to have children but decides against it. Why must these couples be careful to run their reasons for not having children through the grid of selfishness?

2. THIS IS NOT THE KIND OF WORLD I WANT TO BRING A CHILD INTO: There are a couple of currently popular objections to not having children. This is one of them. But, in the words of this chapter, "We should not let the erosion of our culture prevent us from having children and trusting God to use them to make a difference" (p. 190). Talk about the following questions with your group:

  a. What fears do you have about raising your kids in the 1990s?

  b. Are things really worse now than they were two thousand years ago? (For a perspective on this, read Romans 1:26-32 and 1 Corinthians 5:1.)

  c. How do you know that your children won't make a significant contribution to changing the world? What if the parents of Jonas Salk, Billy Graham, or Abraham Lincoln had felt that way?

3. WE CAN'T AFFORD TO HAVE CHILDREN RIGHT NOW. "Let me bottom-line my response to this objection. When people say they can't afford kids, too many times I think what they are really saying is, 'If we have kids, we will have to lower our standard of living'" (p. 191). Discuss these questions with one another.

  a. What do you think is behind an attitude like this?

  b. Have you ever known a couple that waited too late to have kids and lived to regret it? Describe what that was like for them.

4. DEALING WITH A CURE FOR OUR SELFISHNESS. "It's been my experience that those who are willing to give up the immediate gratification that comes from choosing a childless marriage quickly see a change taking place in their lives once a baby shows up. The change is this: God begins dealing with your own selfishness by giving you someone to care for who is infinitely more selfish than you" (p. 195). Talk with one another about these questions.

a. Reread page 196 through the first paragraph of page 197. What are some examples like this from your life where God has taught you about your own selfishness? What lessons have you learned?

b. Yes, having children is a sacrifice. Are the results worth it? Why?

CHAPTER NINE

How to Raise Masculine Sons and Feminine Daughters

Taking Aim at These Issues

1. REALIZING OUR CHILDREN'S SEXUAL IDENTITY IS AT STAKE.
"Confusion over the meaning of sexual personhood is epidemic. . . . The consequence . . . is more divorce, more homosexuality, more sexual abuse, more promiscuity, . . . and more emotional distress and suicide that comes with the loss of God-given identity" (p. 201). Toss these questions around for a minute.

   a. Think of each of your kids right now. What if one or more of them came to you and said, "Dad, I'm gay," or "Dad, I'm pregnant." How would you feel?

   b. How confident are you that your children will

be able to avoid sexual sin? What are you *actively* doing right now to insure they can and will?

c. If a prostitute, junkie, or homosexual showed up on your doorstep and asked for ten hours a week with your children to talk about their lifestyle, would you let them in? Are you letting them in through the television?

2. HOW TO RAISE A HOMOSEXUAL. "I pastored for ten years in the San Francisco Bay area and counseled with more than a few homosexuals. You would be surprised at how many can quote verse after verse from the Bible. It's shocking to realize how many of them were raised in Christian homes. . . . In every case I have seen where they were so raised, their fathers were either spiritually anorexic or bulimic" (p. 202-203). Discuss this with your group.

a. How does it make you feel to think that your children's sexual identities and moral characters are, in a large degree, dependent on *your* spiritual health? What does that realization make you want to do?

b. How often do you pray for your kids' moral purity and sexual identity? Brainstorm with the guys in your group about what the content of those prayers should be. (Use these passages if you need some ideas: Leviticus 20:10-21; Proverbs 5; 1 Corinthians 6:15-20; 2 Corinthians 6:14-18; Philippians 4:8; 1 Thessalonians 4:3-7; 2 Timothy 2:20-22; Hebrews 13:4.) Use the space below for things you want to remember.

_____

_____

_____

3. A CHILD'S SEXUAL HEALTH DEPENDS ON DAD. "In gender role development, the evidence points to fathers as having the more important influence, not only in fostering a male self-concept in boys, but femininity in girls. . . ." (pp. 204-205). Discuss these questions with the group.

    a. Did you grow up with any confusion about male and female roles? In what ways were you confused? Has any of that affected your relationships with your wife or kids? What important lessons have these experiences taught you about proper male and female roles?

    b. Did you grow up with any confusion or bad influence about healthy, biblical sexual relationships? How has that affected your sex life now? What lessons have you learned about sex that you want your kids to know?

    c. If you came from a home that gave you clear, biblical values on these issues, share how that has affected you as an adult. What things did your parents teach you that you're most thankful for?

4. RAISING OUR CHILDREN IN FAIRNESS. "Habitual unfairness over the years results in an accumulation of anger that eventually embitters children toward their father. 'A child frequently irritated by overseverity or injustice, to which, nevertheless, it must submit, acquires a spirit of sullen resignation, leading to despair.' What a terrible way to grow up!" (pp. 206-207). Toss these questions around for a minute.

    a. Some of you know what all of this is like because that's the way it was when you were a boy. Describe that experience for the group and then talk about how it affects you today. Also, talk about this: What things did your father do that you've sworn you'll never do?

b. As hard as it is to believe, it's often true that children from hard or abusive backgrounds will repeat the same mistakes when raising *their* children. If you came from an abusive situation, how can you keep that from happening in your home?

c. This chapter talks about six ways a father can embitter his children. He can

- be over-protective.

- play favorites.

- habitually discourage them.

- forget the child is growing up, has a right to his own ideas, and does not need to be a replica of his father.

- neglect them.

- use bitter words and physical cruelty.

Which of these are the easiest for you to fall into? Why? Which have you had success avoiding? Share your success with the other guys. (If you hear something that might help you in one of these areas, jot it down on the lines below.)

_____

_____

_____

5. RAISING OUR CHILDREN WITH TENDERNESS. "Our boys and girls need dads who are tuned into them. They need dads who are interested in the stuff of their lives. *They need dads who will listen before they spank.* They need dads who will give them plenty of hugs and kisses" (p. 211). Discuss these things for a few minutes.

a. Think of someone you've known who was tender. What's an action they took toward you that you remember as tender? If you could come up with a list of adjectives to describe that person, what would be on the list?

b. Most of us tend to think that tenderness isn't very masculine. Why? Can you think of some "real men" in Scripture who were tender? Use these verses for reference: Genesis 45:1-15; 2 Samuel 9; John 11:30-44; 1 Thessalonians 2:5-9.)

c. Can you think of instances in which God has demonstrated His tenderness? You may use the following verses to help in your discussion: Isaiah 40:9-11; Hosea 11:1-4; Psalm 103; 145:8-9; Luke 1:76-79; Ephesians 4:32.

d. This section talks about four ways to be tender with kids.

• Listen to them and respect their feelings.

• Clearly admit any wrongdoing toward them and ask their forgiveness.

• Listen to your wife's input about each child.

• Be "high touch" and dispense liberal doses of encouragement to them (and don't forget your wife while you're at it).

Which of these is the easiest for you? Why? Which is hardest? Why? As a group, come up with three practical suggestions for how to make each principle operational in your home. Use the following spaces for notes.

1. Listening and respect _____

_____

_____

2. Admitting fault and asking forgiveness_____

_____

_____

3. Listening to my wife_____

_____

_____

4. "High touch" and encouragement_____

_____

_____

6. *RAISING OUR CHILDREN WITH FIRMNESS.* "A father's task is many-sided, but the most important part of his work is to fit himself and his children into God's plan of family authority. . . . To refuse to discipline a child is to refuse a clear demand of God, for a child who doesn't learn to obey both parents will find it much harder to learn to obey God." (p. 216). Talk about these questions with one another.

    a. Do you take the lead in matters of discipline in the home, or do you leave it to your wife? (All of us have been guilty of that at times.) Why? What does Ephesians 6:4 say about this?

    b. It's hard to balance firmness and tenderness. Most of us tend toward one extreme or the other. Which way do you usually lean? Why? What are some factors that tend to throw you out of balance?

    c. What are some tips you can offer one another

about how to know if you're balanced? Use the space below to record the good ideas you hear.

_____

_____

_____

7. RAISING OUR CHILDREN IN CHRIST. Reread pages 218 and 219 on this section and then talk about this question.

How can you know if you're under the quality control of the Holy Spirit? How can you know if you're out of control? Use the spaces below for notes.

_____

_____

_____

8. THE RESULTS OF FOLLOWING THE LANDMARKS. What happens when a son and daughter have a dad who's moral compass is properly calibrated and who gives them just the right balance of fairness, tenderness, and firmness—all under the quality control of Christ? *"The result is a child who not only has a clear sexual identity but also has a backpack chock-full of healthy self-confidence"* (p. 219).

a. Think of a family you've known whose kids have exhibited these traits. What have you learned from watching those parents that can help you be a better parent?

b. All of us need help to be successful parents. What's stopping you from asking the parents you just mentioned (or another couple you know) to be an ongoing resource for you—a couple you could talk to, share ideas with, pray with, etc? If you don't have anyone like that, ask the guys in your group to pray that God would bring a couple like that into your lives.

Telling Your Kids What You Don't Want to Tell Them

Taking Aim at These Issues

1. THERE ARE A LOT OF PEOPLE OUT THERE WHO WANT TO TELL OUR KIDS ABOUT SEX. "Let's put the cards on the table. A war is raging for our children, and Planned Parenthood and its philosophical cousins are the enemy. They are trying to rip apart everything that remains that is right, moral, godly, and decent. And they are walking into our public schools every day with the intention of undercutting the value system of Christian parents" (p. 227). Talk about this with the other guys.

    a. Reread page 224 through the top of page 226. Do you know what kind of sex education your children are getting in school? If not, why not?

b. Suppose it were your daughter telling the story related on these pages. How would you handle a situation like that?

2. *THERE'S NOTHING TO BE EMBARRASSED ABOUT.* "Maybe the thought of talking to your son about sex embarrasses you. Allow me to suggest that although you may feel some embarrassment, there is nothing to be embarrassed about. As Dr. Howard Hendricks expresses it, 'We should not be ashamed to discuss that which God was not ashamed to create' " (p. 227).

a. Are you ashamed or embarrassed to talk with your kids about sex? Why? Why not? If you are, what do you think would most help you get over your embarrassment?

b. Did your parents tell you about sex? If not, who did? How has that affected your views on sex?

3. *A MAN IS RESPONSIBLE TO TEACH HIS KIDS ABOUT SEX.* "As a rule of thumb, fathers should teach their sons and mothers should teach their daughters. But the father, as head of the family, has a responsibility to make sure that each child is given the proper and correct instruction by the appropriate parent at the right time" (p. 228).

a. Have you made any decisions about when you'll discuss what with your kids? Why? Why not?

b. What facet of discussing sex with your son(s) most worries you?

4. *GETTING TO YOUR KIDS BEFORE THEIR PEERS DO.* "If your child is ten, let me assure you that he knows more than you think he knows. He has already gotten the information. The only question is, from whom did he get it and how accurate is it?" (p. 234). Think about these questions with one another.

   a. Suppose your children came up to you today and asked you about sex. Keeping in mind their age, what would you tell them? How would you tell them? What wouldn't you tell them? Why?

   b. Some of your kids may have already "heard it through the grapevine." How accurate was their information? How much did it reflect God's perspective? Do you regret not having been the one to first tell them about it? Why?

   c. Assuming your children don't know about sex yet, decide right now, with the group, when you're going to tell each child. Before you put your plan into action, *make sure you talk with your wife first.*

5. A PLAN FOR HOW TO TALK TO YOUR CHILDREN. "When [you] sit down to talk with [your] son, . . . you want to be impromptu, but you also want to be prepared" (p. 235).

   a. Do you feel prepared to talk with your children? If not, what are some practical things you can do to be more prepared?

   b. This chapter suggests eight guidelines to follow when talking to your kids about sex.

   • Small questions deserve small answers.

   • Big questions deserve big answers.

   • Frank questions deserve frank answers.

   • Be casual and natural.

   • Look for teachable moments.

   • Use the right terms without embarrassment.

- Consider your child's age.
- Let them know they can ask you anything and get a straight answer.

If you need to go back and review any of these, they're discussed on pages 236 to 241.

c. Is there anything else you'd add to the list?

d. Assuming you haven't talked with your children about sex, which of these do you think will be easy for you to do? Why? Which will be difficult? Why?

e. If you have talked with them, which of these did you have the most success with? Why? Where did you struggle? Why? If you could do it over again, what would you do differently?

f. If your parents told you about sex, think back about that conversation and others you had with them over the years. What did they do that really helped you? Is there anything they did that didn't help?

CHAPTER ELEVEN

Rock and Role Model

Taking Aim at These Issues

1. THE BALL OF LEADERSHIP IS IN THE BABY-BOOMERS' COURT.
"We have become the people of influence in America. . . .
When we were kids we would often get upset about
the way our parents handled things. Now we are the
parents, and we get to make the decisions. And the
decisions we make with our power and influence will
have a tremendous impact on the next generation" (p.
252). Discuss these things with the group.

    a. When you were a teenager, what were some of
       the things you swore you'd do differently than
       your parents? Are you? Why or why not?

    b. How has your perspective changed over the

years about what's really important and of real value in life? What factors have changed your perspective?

c. Describe the kind of legacy you want to leave to your family and others who are important to you. Describe the legacy you'd like our generation (the baby boomers) to leave for our society.

2. GEARING UP FOR OUR MIDLIFE CRISIS. "We male baby boomers are entering a difficult period of our lives. We must come to grips with the fact that our youthfulness is vanishing with every passing day. Some of us are going to stall in our careers, . . . chuck our jobs, leave our families, buy a red Mazda Miata and a few gold chains, and try to cover our bald spots as we think about asking out the new twenty-three-year-old receptionist" (p. 253). Talk about these questions for a few minutes.

a. Twenty-five years ago "midlife crisis" wasn't in our vocabulary. Why has there been an explosion of concern and attention paid to it in recent years?

b. What's at the heart of a midlife crisis? What's the cure for one?

c. Have you ever known anyone who's gone through a midlife crisis? What was it like for them? What did they learn?

d. What's to keep you from doing some of the things listed above? If you could come up with a list of three things you think would help you weather the storm of a midlife crisis, what would be on it? (Use the following spaces to take notes on things you want to remember that the other guys say):

_____

_____

_____

_____

3. BEING MEN WHO ARE ROCKS. "God is looking for men between twenty-five and forty-five who will commit to be "rocks" for their families. These kind of rocks are characterized by an unwavering commitment to their wives, a willingness to get involved in the lives of their children, and a gut-level desire to follow hard after Jesus Christ" (p. 254).

   a. Look at the last sentence above. Three things are mentioned there that characterize a rock. Which of the three presents the biggest challenge for you? Why? What's *one* practical thing you could do in the next three months that would help you make strides in that area?

   Use the space below to list what each guy in the group says about what he wants to do in the next three months. Using that as your prayer list, make a commitment to pray that God would give each guy success. Pray for each individual at least once a week for the next three months.

_____

_____

_____

_____

_____

*I make a steadfast promise to pray for each guy in
my group at least once a week for the next three
months*

_____

Signed

_____

Date

b. If your father wasn't a rock in your life, do you
   know why? What did you miss out on the most
   because he wasn't?

c. For those of you who's dad *wasn't* a rock,
   what's the biggest challenge you face being
   that rock for your family? What would you
   most like help with? From whom?

d. If your dad *was* a rock, what made him that
   way? What are some of the specific things he
   did that you want to model in your life?

4. KNOWING CHRIST IS THE ROLE MODEL WE NEED. "None of
us have had perfect role models, and none of us will
be perfect role models. . . . Every one of us must realize that Jesus Christ is our personal rock and personal
role model" (p. 256).

a. If most of us are honest, we'd admit we often
   look to another human being as our role model
   instead of Christ. What are the dangers in
   doing that?

b. Most of us would also admit that, at times, it's
   pretty intimidating to try to copy Christ. After
   all, He's perfect! Read Hebrews 2:17-18 and
   4:14-16 and discuss what those verses say.

c. What one role does Christ have that provides
   us with a model of what we should be like?

(Use these verses to help pinpoint the answer: Mark 10:45; John 4:34 and 5:30; Ephesians 5:25; Philippians 2:5-8.)

d. Using the following scale, rate yourself on servanthood.

1	2	3	4	5	6	7	8	9	10

dedicated to serving   dedicated to serving
myself   others

Share your answer with the other guys. What's one thing you could do in the next few weeks that would move your score closer to a ten?

Steve Farrar speaks to thousands of people each year in evangelical churches across North America. His well-known conference, "Building Strong Families," is recognized as one of the foremost equipping tools for families in America today. A native Californian and a pastor for fifteen years, Steve is president of Strategic Living Ministries in Dallas, Texas. He is a graduate of California State University, Fullerton, and Western Seminary in Portland, Oregon. He also holds an earned doctorate from Dallas Theological Seminary. Steve and his wife, Mary, have three children, Rachel, John, and Joshua.